Organizing for Change: New Priorities for Community Colleges

Organizing for Change: New Priorities for Community Colleges

David S. Bushnell

Senior Staff Scientist, Human Resources Research Organization
formerly Director of Research, Project Focus,
American Association of Community and Junior Colleges

McGraw-Hill Book Company

New York	*Kuala Lumpur*	*Panama*
St. Louis	*London*	*Rio de Janeiro*
San Francisco	*Mexico*	*Singapore*
Düsseldorf	*Montreal*	*Sydney*
Johannesburg	*New Delhi*	*Toronto*

Library of Congress Cataloging in Publication Data

Bushnell, David S.
    Organizing for Change.

    Report of a study project, Project Focus, initiated
by the American Association of Junior Colleges.
    Includes bibliographical references.
    1. Municipal junior colleges—United States.
I. American Association of Junior Colleges. II. Title.
LB2328.B86   378.1'543   72-10908
ISBN 0-07-009311-3

Organizing for Change: New Priorities for Community Colleges

This book is based on "A Report From Project
Focus: Strategies for Change," prepared for
the American Association of Community and Junior
Colleges by David S. Bushnell and Ivars Zageris.

1 2 3 4 5 6 7 8 9 0 EBEB 7 9 8 7 6 5 4 3

*The editors for this book were Paul
Walker and Alice V. Manning, the designer was
Marsha Cohen, and its production was super-
vised by James E. Lee. It was set in Century
by Port City Press.
It was printed and bound by Edwards Brothers
Incorporated.*

To the two women in my life,
my mother and my wife

Contents

List of Charts

List of Tables

Acknowledgments

On behalf of the Project Focus team, I wish to acknowledge the valuable support offered by various agencies during the study. We are particularly indebted to the American College Testing Program, Inc., and to Dr. Phil Rever, whose survey experience and data processing skills were invaluable. ACT's willingness to permit us to use the Institutional Self-Study Survey form and manuals enabled us to be sure that the data collected would be both reliable and valid. Dr. Fred Harcleroad, president of ACT, was most helpful in making the considerable resources of ACT available to us.

The Educational Testing Service—in particular, Richard Peterson and Elden Park—was a substantial contributor to the success of this undertaking. With ETS's permission and the assistance of Dr. William Turnbull, president of ETS, the Institutional Goals Inventory was modified for use in our survey.

The National Center for Educational Statistics of the U.S. Office of Education, under the direction of Dorothy Gilford, was instrumental in providing a grant that made it possible for us to obtain information on students currently enrolled. We are grateful to Richard Berry and Eugene Tucker for facilitating and monitoring the contract.

A number of other groups advised and counseled the research staff during the formative stages of the study. The Berkeley Center for Higher Education Research and the Bureau of Social Science Research in Washington, D.C., merit particular mention. A number of their staff members served as valuable sounding boards. Others were asked to review and comment on portions of the manuscript. In particular, I wish to thank Max Raines and Gunder Myran of Michigan State University, James Wattenbarger of the University of Florida, Edward Gross of the University of Washington, Richard Peterson of ETS, and Ray Schultz and Roger Yarrington of AACJC for their willingness to read and comment upon various chapters of the report.

The author is indebted to Ronald Havelock and Thomas Cottingim for their counsel and creative insights into the problems of planned change. Dr. Cottingim's doctoral dissertation, scheduled for publication soon under the tentative title *Management of Change in the Community College*, examines in great detail the problems of introducing change into community colleges.

John Creager of the American Council on Education provided

valuable assistance in designing the sampling procedures and suggesting appropriate weighting procedures. Vernon Hendrick served as a consultant to the project during the earlier phases of designing the sample and structuring the questionnaires. Several staff members of AACJC provided counsel and encouragement throughout the study. Aikin Connor and William Inglis gave us the benefit of their experience and knowledge of computer programming. Barbara Koziarz served as editorial advisor and made many helpful improvements in the wording of the report. During the project, Edith Liebske, Dollie Baggett, Brenda Warren, and Margaret Takanaka provided the staff support and dedication necessary to bring the report to its conclusion. Melody Wood typed and proofread most of the final manuscript. To her and other members of the staff I am forever indebted.

Ivars Zageris provided valuable assistance in many phases of the study. He proved to be particularly helpful in the statistical treatment of the data. I also wish to acknowledge the many contributions of Francis Pray, Donald Beckley, and other members of Frantzreb and Pray Associates, Inc. Their cooperation during some of the more hectic periods surrounding the field visits is very much appreciated.

Finally, Edmund J. Gleazer, Jr., as director of the project, kept before us the objectives of the study and stressed the importance of firsthand observations in making sense out of the data. His ability to interpret and to find the significant connections between what was observed and the causes was inspiring.

These are the people who helped to ensure that the insights gained through Project Focus would be valid and would have a bearing upon the future role of community junior colleges. It goes almost without saying that the errors of commission and omission over which the reader may stumble as he reads through this manuscript are those of the author and not his associates.

David S. Bushnell

Foreword

Perhaps no educational institution has recently been the subject of more discussion, optimistic predictions, and glowing pronouncements than the American two-year college. Nor in fact is it likely that any institution is more eligible for such attention. While its promise was apparent early in the twentieth century, each succeeding decade has revealed its increasing importance in extending educational opportunity. While at one time it might have been regarded as a stepchild, it is now accepted as an integral part of postsecondary education. Moreover, the Carnegie Commission on Higher Education has estimated that between 230 and 280 new public community colleges will be needed by 1980 in order to serve the increasing number and diversity of students who will seek admission to these institutions.

As one who had the privilege (slightly more than ten years ago) of making a study and reporting on the community college, I discussed in the last chapter of *The Junior College: Progress and Prospect* some of the issues which these institutions would probably face during the decade of the 1960s. My concluding paragraph reads as follows:

> It will soon be a hundred years since the two-year college was conceived. There were realistic expectations that have been fulfilled, and there were also overexpectations. The next ten years will sharpen and identify whatever role it is to have in the future.

In hindsight one might conclude that my generalization was a bit premature. Although the role of these institutions was indeed sharpened during the 1960s, the identification of its eventual role was still unclear at the end of the decade.

In any event, in 1970 the W. K. Kellogg Foundation made funds available for another nationwide study of the community college, now known as *Project Focus*. The purpose of this study was to determine where community colleges are headed, how likely they are to reach their objectives, and what alternative strategies ought to be considered. It was the hope that the various recommendations emanating from the study would serve as policy guides for the American Association of Community and Junior Colleges (AACJC) and its institutional members.

This book, authored by David S. Bushnell, is one of three publications to emerge from the study. A companion publication reports Edmund J. Gleazer, Jr.'s firsthand impressions of significant events in the field, gathered during his extensive 10-month tour, in which he interviewed 1,500 persons located in 30 institutions in 20 states. A third report, already published, contains a set of recommendations for change in the scope and function of the American Association of Community and Junior Colleges.

Readers of this volume are certain to be informed by the carefully planned and executed research in which the backgrounds, feelings, and expectations of students as well as faculty were analyzed and compared. Of even greater significance are the author's delineations of the priorities and problems facing community colleges, and the elucidation of a strategy for change that may well be *the* goal for the 1970s.

Students of the community college as well as those with decision-making responsibilities will do well to consider seriously the content of this publication, particularly the suggestions for effecting change. The community colleges have gained much ground in the last few years, but in these times of financial crisis and public concern about postsecondary education generally, they cannot be complacent about their current status. Forces from both within and without are raising many questions concerning both their structure and their program, and the recognition they have gained could be lost unless they demonstrate unusual flexibility and adaptability in a period of rapid social change.

Leland L. Medsker

Organizing for Change: New Priorities for Community Colleges

Chapter I.
Introduction

Seventy-two years ago, eight junior colleges existed in this country, with a total enrollment of approximately 100 students. By 1971, 1,100 private and public two-year colleges were flourishing, with over 2,500,000 enrollees. [1][1] The prospects for continued growth through 1980 are strong. Where this national movement is headed and what and how students will be served are already being determined by the play of forces now in motion. By tapping the views of trustees, community leaders, faculty members, key administrators, and students; by assessing current population and economic trends; and by drawing upon other research efforts, we hoped to identify and analyze the forces influencing the future direction of community and junior colleges and draw empirically valid conclusions.

The study was funded by the W. K. Kellogg Foundation, a major supporter of community and junior colleges, in the hope that it would aid those responsible for directing the nation's effort in achieving the unique goals set for these institutions. Its primary purpose was to determine the extent to which community and junior colleges are actually enrolling a broad cross section of students through such mechanisms as an open-door policy, occupational education programs, career guidance services, college transfer pro-

[1] All references will be listed at the back of the report. Specific page references will be given in the text.

1

grams, and community outreach efforts. Such policies and programs require a careful assessment at this time if desired changes or minor corrections in the community junior colleges are to be achieved by the end of the decade.

This study had four major objectives. First, representatives of key constituent groups were to be polled to determine their views on the long-range goals to be served. Second, discrepancies between the desired goals and the present situation were to be pinpointed. Third, social and economic trends likely to influence the future direction of community and junior colleges during this decade were to be identified. Fourth, a set of strategies for systematically achieving greater harmony between goals and current practice were to be set forth. To obtain the information necessary to achieve these objectives, a literature search was conducted and communication links with already existing data banks on community junior colleges were established. Through the use of structured interviews, survey questionnaires, and site visits, relevant data were obtained from a nationwide sample of community junior colleges. An advisory group was convened in the early stages of the project to solicit reactions to the areas being probed by the questionnaires and interviews, and to suggest various hypotheses for testing once the data were in. This group met in early February 1971. Their deliberation had a profound impact upon the subsequent analysis.

A small team of three professionals and two assistants took upon themselves the responsibility for gathering and interpreting the necessary data. An outside consulting firm, Frantzreb and Pray Associates, Inc., was asked to conduct a special analysis, within the larger framework, in order to recommend changes in the organizational structure and services of the AACJC. Dr. Edmund J. Gleazer, Jr., executive director of the AACJC, took a year's leave of absence from the association and assumed primary responsibility for the conduct of the field study. As director of the project, he was also responsible for the overall interpretation of the data and for the recommendations of the Project Focus Task Force. David S. Bushnell was given responsibility for the research activities involved in the preparation of this report. Ivars Zageris served as staff associate.

SAMPLE SELECTION

The first step in the study was to identify the population of community and junior colleges to be sampled. Two-year postsecondary institutions have been variously labeled "community colleges," "junior colleges," "branch colleges," etc. Most are supported by a local school district, either in conjunction with the elementary and secondary schools or as a separate junior college district. Others derive their support from the state or operate as privately funded institutions with most of their income derived from tuition.[2] The *1970 Junior College Directory*, published by the American Association of Community and Junior Colleges, was adopted as the operational definition of the population to be studied. The number of community junior colleges listed in the *Directory* is somewhat larger than that reported by the U.S. Office of Education. This is due primarily to the fact that AACJC includes in its membership two-year branch campuses who elected to become members of the association. Not all institutions listed in the *Directory*, however, are members of AACJC. Those branch campuses which are integral parts of their respective parent institutions and do not function as community junior colleges were excluded from the population to be sampled. Fifty-six campuses from the states of Ohio, Pennsylvania, South Carolina, and Wisconsin were eliminated for this reason. In addition, for logistic reasons, only colleges in the continental United States were considered, thus excluding colleges in Alaska, Hawaii, Puerto Rico, etc. After establishing these two qualifications, 956 community junior colleges remained to be sampled. Of these, 721 were public institutions, 107 were independent junior colleges, and 128 were private church-related junior colleges.

Survey instruments were mailed to the selected institutions. Students, faculty, and presidents each completed separate instruments. An institutional questionnaire was also administered to provide basic data on the institutions involved. Copies of the four questionnaires can be found in Appendix B. The data presented in this report are derived primarily from the findings from the questionnaires. Occasionally, when a particular interpretation of the data was open to question, we drew upon the extensive interview material gathered by Dr. Gleazer and other members of the staff during their visits to a subsample of institutions drawn from the larger sample.

---

[2] Throughout this report, "community colleges" will refer to the public two-year colleges. The term "junior colleges," on the other hand, has come to mean privately supported institutions, both sectarian and nonsectarian. This distinction will be maintained throughout the report. "Community junior colleges" will encompass both types of institution.

METHODOLOGY

A two-stage sampling design was used. The first stage involved a stratified sample of colleges drawn from the *1970 Directory*. The second stage involved a random selection of respondents (students and faculty) within the selected institutions. Various weights were assigned to make the estimates of population parameters from the data obtained in the survey (Appendix A describes the weighting procedures employed).

The institutions listed in the *1970 Directory* were stratified according to geographic area, size, and type: public, church-related, or independent. Because of the small number of institutions falling into the church-related and independent junior college classifications, these groups were not broken down any further. The public community colleges were classified into six geographic regions, corresponding to those developed by Vernon Hendrix in his 1965 study [37] of the impact of the two-year college environment on students. The regions were selected in such a way that no single state would dominate a given region, with the exception of California, which was made into a separate region. The regions encompassed economically and essentially culturally homogeneous areas. Within each region, colleges were classified according to size. The complete stratification resulted in 32 cells to be used for sampling purposes (see Table 3*a*, Appendix A).

A 10 percent random sample was drawn from each cell. No cell was left at zero; each cell had at least one entry. Thus, due to rounding, the overall percentage was slightly higher than 10 percent. The initial sample consisted of 100 institutions.

The presidents of the sample institutions were contacted by letter during the latter part of January 1971. Twenty-one presidents turned down the initial invitation to participate. As soon as a rejection was received, the institution was replaced with another randomly chosen from the same cell. At the time of the cutoff date (March 26, 1971), 92 institutions had agreed to participate in the study. This constituted the final sample. The overall match of actual against desired cell frequencies is reported in Table 3*a*, Appendix A. Table 4*a*, Appendix A, demonstrates that the 21 refusals were randomly distributed, with no one geographic area dominating. In addition, three institutions failed to advise us of their inability to participate before the cutoff date, thus bringing the total number of initially sampled nonparticipants to 24. Follow-up letters and individual telephone calls helped to ensure that the overall rate of participation was more than adequate.

STUDENT SAMPLE

Each president who agreed to participate in the study was asked to appoint a member of his immediate staff to coordinate the administration of questionnaires to students and faculty. The campus coordinators were given instructions on sample-selection procedures and on the appropriate steps to follow when administering the questionnaires. The importance of ensuring the confidentiality of the results was emphasized. Each coordinator was asked to select a random sample of students on the following basis: If the institution had less than 1,000 full-time students, 100 students should be selected for inclusion in the survey. If the institution had more than 1,000 but less than 10,000 students, a 10 percent random sample was to be selected. If the institution had 10,000 or more students, a 5 percent random sample was to be selected. Only full-time students were to be included. One of three alternative sampling procedures outlined in the American College Testing Program Manual [3] was to be employed. Each campus coordinator was instructed to ensure that the ratio of freshmen to sophomores at each institution would be properly reflected in the sample chosen. From an initial sample of 12,022, 10,250 student responses were accepted as usable, giving us a response rate of 85.6 percent. By assigning the proper weights, this sample was generalized to a total weighted population of 1,133,916 students. It is this figure which serves as our base line for the subsequent analysis.

FACULTY SAMPLE

The faculty were sampled in much the same way as the students. Each coordinator was instructed to select a 10 percent random sample of faculty members if the institution had more than 500 full-time faculty. Those institutions which had fewer than 500 were instructed to survey 50 randomly drawn faculty members or, if less than 50 were employed, all were to complete the questionnaire.

The number of faculty members was based upon the number of full-time, certified faculty members plus those administrators who primarily teach but also serve as deans and department chairmen. For the most part, questionnaires were distributed to the faculty by campus mail and returned to the campus coordinator in sealed envelopes.

The total number of faculty sampled initially was 2,741; there were 2,491 usable faculty responses, or a response rate of 90.9 percent. The weighted population of faculty came to 69,350. Since both student and faculty response rates were so high, no special study of nonrespondents was conducted.

In addition to being assigned the responsibility for designing and selecting an appropriate sample of students and faculty, the campus coordinator was asked to complete the institutional questionnaire. Unfortunately, because of the difficulty encountered in completing this questionnaire, relatively few coordinators were able to complete this assignment in the time allotted. The poor response rate on the institutional survey instrument led us to abandon the use of this questionnaire.

Ninety presidents completed their questionnaire, giving us a 98 percent response rate.

The survey team is indebted to the American College Testing Program (ACT) not only for permission to use their Institutional Self-Study Survey form but also for their willingness to commit staff and computer time to the project. They arranged to have the data edited and stored by optical scanning equipment, and actually programmed and ran a good part of the analysis, with the collaboration of the Project Focus staff.

We are also indebted to the Educational Testing Service (ETS) for the use of their Institutional Goals Inventory. It proved to be the right instrument at the right time. A modified form was employed to comply with the space limitations imposed by the ACT optical scan answer sheets.

In addition to the time, staff resources, and instruments made available by both testing services, the National Center for Educational Statistics (NCES) of the U.S. Office of Education contracted with us to analyze the student data and to provide them with a series of tables summarizing the results of our analysis. NCES is in the process of publishing a brief description and summary of the data on community junior college students made available through the auspices of Project Focus.

Chapter 2.
The Warp and Woof of Junior Colleges: Students and Faculty

The unprecedented growth of public community colleges during the last decade—a 300 percent increase in enrollments and a doubling of the number of institutions—attests to the popularity of these remarkable institutions. Twenty years ago community colleges were being asked to prove themselves worthy of the name of higher education. Even as recently as 1964, Robert Hutchins described the community college movement as "confused, confusing, and contradictory. It has something for everybody. It is generous, ignoble, bold, timid, naive, and optimistic . . . its heart is in the right place; its head does not work very well." [39] Others see it as "one of the few unique accomplishments of American Education in the 20th Century." [20] As a mainstay of mass higher education, community junior colleges have emerged as a true melting pot for the community. Their unique function has been chronicled by many but critically evaluated by few. The verdict is not yet in on how well they have succeeded in the tougher tasks of higher education. However, the data will demonstrate that progress is being made.

Founded initially as a place where eligible students could enroll in two years of lower-division undergraduate study, the community-based public two-year college has expanded its purposes to encompass a variety of community, cultural, and educational needs. Its three traditional functions—transfer, terminal, and community service—were first laid down by Lange, [44] Koos, [42] and others as early as 1927. These classical functions are still as relevant today as they were fifty years ago. Bogue's book *The Community College*, [8] published in 1950, introduced the concept of the public community college as a third force in education, providing a fresh approach and a needed antidote to the traditional curricula of high school and college.

Even before Bogue, the Truman Commission on Higher Education [56] noted the need for expanded educational opportunities beyond high school. According to their scores on the Army General Classification Tests, 49 percent of those conscripted for military service during the war years qualified for fourteen years of education; 32 percent were found to be qualified for four years of college; and 16 percent were qualified for graduate study. The Commission concluded that "the time has come to make education through the fourteenth grade available in the same way that high school is now available."

Opening the doors to higher education for all candidates, regardless of race, religion, or wealth, was at that time a revolutionary idea. Since then the goal of many states (recently reinforced by the Carnegie Commission on Higher Education [14]) has been to put a college within commuting distance of every potential enrollee. Willingham, [70] in his detailed state-by-state examination of the need for additional educational institutions, demonstrates that if the number of new community colleges continues to grow at its present rate in the right places, universal higher education through the fourteenth year for 90 percent of the population of this country will become a reality by 1980.

More recently, the civil rights movement has mounted a major effort to open up postsecondary educational opportunities to minorities and to disadvantaged students generally. Massive investments by state governments, backed up to a lesser extent by federal appropriations, have helped local institutions reach out and involve these "new" students. The establishment of state master plans for higher education (patterned after California's master plan) introduced a number of new alternatives for the marginal students that have helped to change the traditional concept of higher education. Technical institutes, area vocational schools, and comprehensive community colleges represent such a range of options at the postsecondary level.

While many disadvantaged and minority students are being provided with financial aid through federally guaranteed loans and Educational Opportunity Grants, some are still having difficulty in finding adequate financial support. A number of studies [6] have shown that the higher a student's socioeconomic background, the more likely he is to attend college and to graduate. Even direct student aid programs have been shown to favor those who come from higher-income families. [33] Whether or not such inequalities are attributable to economic or social factors has yet to be conclusively demonstrated; however, the inequities persist.

Most advocates of the open-door college support the concept of free tuition at least through the first two years of college. The Educational Policies Commission of the N.E.A. recommended in 1964 that a tuition-free education for the first two years beyond high school be provided to all students seeking it. [26] The Carnegie Commission more recently recommended a similar goal, namely, that no tuition be charged for the first two years of a college education at a public institution. [17] The continuing pressure to expand access to higher education is the product of many forces. Low cost/low risk institutions appeal to students who could not otherwise afford college or to those who are undecided on their future careers. The accessibility of most community colleges to both college-age and adult enrollees creates a unique institutional appeal. Local employers seeking trained workers view it as an economic asset. Civic leaders look to it for cultural enrichment.

However, not all observers of the educational scene give the community colleges their unalloyed endorsement. Christopher Jencks and David Riesman, in *The Academic Revolution,* [40] attribute the popularity of the public community college to proximity, low cost, and a backlash against nationally oriented colleges and universities. Much of this backlash, they contend, reflects the anxiety of lower-middle-class parents about the increasing emancipation of the younger generation on the residential campus. Because the universities have become increasingly selective, these same parents want to be sure that their own offspring have access to higher education without the sacrifices and demands imposed by four-year institutions. It is the Jencks and Riesman thesis that community colleges appeal primarily to the marginal student of modest ability and uncertain plans. How well their observations are borne out by today's mix of community college students will be examined shortly.

Frank Newman [52, p. 71] sums up the dilemma confronting the nation's community junior colleges by observing that

the public and especially the four-year colleges are shifting more and more of the responsibility onto the two-year colleges for undertaking the toughest tasks of higher education. Simultaneously, the problems we have already identified—the poor match between the students' style of learning and the institutions' style of teaching, the lock step pressure to attend college directly after high school, the overemphasis on credentials—are overtaking the community colleges and rendering them increasingly ill equipped to perform the immense task they have been given.

Whatever the shortcomings of community junior colleges, enrollment expansion continues unabated. At the time of the Truman Commission, about 25 percent of college-age students were actually enrolled in college. By 1980, the percentage is expected to have swelled to 66 percent. The Carnegie Commission announced recently that freshmen enrollment in public and private four-year institutions declined in 1971 when compared with 1970 levels. Two-year colleges, on the other hand, experienced an 8 percent increase in total enrollment. Students from racial minority groups were reported to have made substantial enrollment gains over 1970. The increase in black and Spanish-surname students in the junior colleges was roughly twice the total enrollment increase at public four-year colleges. In the words of Pat Cross, [23, p. 1] "we are no longer concerned with whether students are ready for higher education, but whether higher education is ready for them."

In this chapter, three important topics will be examined. First, the backgrounds, the expectations, and the reactions of students who participated in our cross-sectional sample of public and private junior colleges will be reported. Second, faculty reactions and perceptions, together with faculty backgrounds and career expectations, will be explored. Third, the contrasting perceptions of students and faculty on various student services and programs will be presented. You will note that the data are presented in the form of national norms so that the reader can more readily generalize from these results to the total population of full-time students and faculty currently involved in our nation's most notable educational experiment.

ENROLLMENT STATISTICS

Of the 2½ million students enrolled, about 50 percent are full time. Many find it necessary to work while attending college. Fifty-four percent of the full-time males and 40 percent of the full-time females work 15 hours a week or more. Approximately two-thirds of the full-time students are freshmen, with 84 percent of this group having graduated from high school in 1970. Only 10 percent of the students live on campus, and over half live at home. Approximately 80 percent applied for admission while living within a 50-mile radius of the college. Roughly half of all the students are from towns or cities of less than 50,000 population. Sixty percent of the students graduated with a high school class of less than 400. Eighty-six percent came to college from a public high school.

The Carnegie Commission report *The Open-Door Colleges* [17, p. 30] revealed that the median enrollment in public community colleges was 1,380, while that for private junior colleges was only 471. Of the public community colleges, 13 percent had enrollments of 5,000 and over, while only 12.6 percent of the private institutions were above the 1,000-enrollment mark. About one out of ten of our sample of full-time students was enrolled in a private junior college.

Statistics such as these illustrate the degree of variability of enrollments at the two-year college level. Public and private two-year colleges do not serve the same constituencies as four-year colleges and universities. The backgrounds and characteristics that shape the interests, career goals, and values of community junior college students are diverse, and there is heavy emphasis on the disadvantaged, the minority, and the home-based student. While these characteristics cannot be changed during a student's college career, they do serve as appropriate background information upon which faculty and administrators can build their strategies for helping students learn. If we think of these factors as "inputs" to the planning process, trends in student characteristics will be helpful to those concerned with predicting future needs. Age, sex, ethnic status, previous high school experiences, and family socioeconomic status are the factors which will be mentioned here.

STUDENT CHARACTERISTICS

Ethnic Status

A dramatic increase in the number of minority group students enrolled full time in public community and private junior colleges is evident when the data from the Project Focus survey are compared with an earlier study (see Table 2.1). Of those responding to the background question on racial or ethnic status in our survey, 31 percent identified themselves as minority group members, compared to only 9 percent in 1969. Out of all students responding, 23 percent are black, 5 percent are Mexican or Spanish-American, 2 percent are

TABLE 2.1   Ethnic group membership by year of enrollment and sex (in percentages)

Ethnic status	1969*		1971†	
	M	F	M	F
Minority	7.5	10.9	33.5	26.8
Nonminority	92.5	89.1	66.5	73.2
Total	100.0	100.0	100.0	100.0

*Based on Bureau of Social Science Research data
†Based on Project Focus data

American Indian, 1 percent are Oriental-American, and the remaining 69 percent identify themselves as Caucasian.[1]

Table 2.2 indicates that fewer minority group members were enrolled as sophomores than were enrolled as freshmen. For example, only 19 percent of the male sophomores were black, while 71 percent were white. The comparatively recent upsurge in black student enrollments in the public community colleges could, of

TABLE 2.2   Enrollment of students by year in school by race and sex (in percentages)

Race	Freshman		Sophomore		Total	
	M	F	M	F	M	F
Afro-American	29.0	22.7	18.9	15.4	25.0	19.8
American Indian	1.5	1.9	2.0	1.6	1.7	1.8
Caucasian	62.8	70.0	71.4	78.7	66.5	73.2
Mexican/Span.-American	5.0	3.8	5.8	4.2	5.3	3.9
Oriental-Am.	1.5	1.5	1.6	1.0	1.5	1.3
Total	99.8	99.9	99.7	99.9	100.0	100.0
(Weighted N in thousands)	(323.0)	(272.7)	(217.8)	(148.9)	(540.8)	(421.6)

[1] Fifteen percent of the student population sampled did not respond to this question, thus raising the issue of the reliability of the distribution as reported. Any subsequent discussion of the findings pertaining to ethnic groups should be viewed with this limitation in mind. Comparisons with a recently reported Census Bureau survey, [66] conducted in October 1970, of currently enrolled undergraduates in two- and four-year institutions, however, confirm the Project Focus data.

course, account for part of this difference. A higher rate of attrition among blacks is the more likely explanation.

Minority students reported lower family incomes than did white students (see Table 2.3). Among males, family income of less than $7,500 a year was reported by 37 percent of the Spanish-surname students, 42 percent of the Afro-Americans, and 48 percent of the American Indians, in contrast with only 18 percent of the Caucasians and 26 percent of the Oriental-Americans. Not all minority group students, however, came from low-income families. Only the Mexican and Spanish-speaking Americans reported that fewer than 20 percent had a family income of $15,000 a year and over. Incidentally, the overall distribution of present family incomes reported by community junior college students closely parallels the national distribution as reported by the U.S. Census. The median income reported in 1970 for all U.S. families was $9,867, [67] almost identical to the median income reported by students participating in the Project Focus survey.

There were few differences among ethnic groups with regard to primary sources of financial support (see Table 2.4). However, more of the male Caucasian and black students depended upon their own employment or personal savings than was the case among male Spanish-surname Americans, American Indians, or Oriental-Americans. More than 28 percent of the female students of American Indian extraction depended on their own employment or savings. The relatively small number of students in this category may account for this apparent deviation, however. One out of every four Oriental-American male students depended upon repayable loans and Educational Opportunity Grants as the principal source of financial support. Almost 20 percent of all male students cited the GI bill or veterans benefits as their principal source of income. Most female students depended upon parents or spouses for support, with the possible exception of the female American Indian cited above.

The educational attainment level of the parents for all ethnic groups was essentially the same, with the possible exception of Spanish-surname students, where a majority reported that their parents had less than a high school diploma. More than half the fathers from each of the ethnic groups were found to have at least a high school education, and 30 percent or more had some college. The educational attainment level of mothers closely paralleled that of fathers in the same group, with the possible exception of mothers of black students, whose overall educational attainment level was higher than the fathers (24 percent of the fathers and 16 percent of the

TABLE 2.3   *Family income by race and sex (in percentages)*

Level of family income	Afro-American American		Mexican/ Spanish-Am.		Caucasian		American Indian		Oriental-American	
	M	F	M	F	M	F	M	F	M	F
$3,000-7,499	42	37	37	42	18	17	48	31	26	24
$7,500-14,900	31	37	36	36	43	33	27	38	40	37
$15,000 and over	21	20	15	6	21	19	14	15	21	21
Don't know	6	6	13	16	19	32	11	16	13	19
Total	100	100	101	100	101	101	100	101	100	101
(Weighted N in thousands)	(138.8)	(82.3)	(27.6)	(16.1)	(352.6)	(302.3)	(9.2)	(7.4)	(8.2)	(5.3)

TABLE 2.4 Primary source of financial support by race and sex (in percentages)

Source of support	Afro-American		Mexican/Spanish-Am.		Caucasian		American Indian		Oriental-American	
	M	F	M	F	M	F	M	F	M	F
Parents or spouse	33	44	34	43	36	56	35	36	49	57
Employment or savings	29	22	19	24	29	19	25	28	15	15
Loan or EOG	10	17	10	17	4	10	10	18	23	7
GI bill	19	6	26	6	19	4	20	6	10	3
Scholarship or grant	6	8	7	7	7	7	6	8	1	8
Other	3	3	4	3	4	3	4	4	2	9
Total	100	100	100	100	99	99	100	100	100	99
(Weighted N in thousands)	(135.8)	(85.3)	(28.9)	(16.5)	(358.4)	(311.1)	(9.1)	(7.2)	(8.3)	(5.6)

mothers were reported to have had an eighth grade education or less).

Most students, regardless of ethnic status, aspired to at least a bachelor's degree (see Table 2.5). Male students consistently aspired to a higher level of educational achievement than did females. Of all female students, 32 percent expected to achieve only an associate of arts degree or a vocational certificate; however, only 16 percent of the male students planned to stop at this level. Among males, 53 percent of the Spanish-surname students and 59 percent of the American Indian students aspired to a master's degree or higher. White, black, and Oriental-American students aspired to about the same educational level, with two out of five indicating a desire for an M.A. degree or higher.

More males than females were enrolled in the college transfer program (see Table 2.6).[2] Only the American Indian female student deviated significantly from the norm. This apparent disinterest in a career education among the various ethnic groups is consistent with earlier studies, [30, p. 71] although the findings may be more apparent than real. Cross comments that: [23, p. 1] "Although it simplifies things to speak of both students enrolled in the technical degree programs and those in the vocational nondegree curricula of the community college as occupationally oriented, it should be noted that many of them say that they hope to transfer to a four-year college." Those students who, one would predict, would be the most likely to benefit from an occupationally oriented curriculum report their reluctance to do so in the not-unfounded fear that if they do not initially enroll in the college transfer program, they will be prevented from doing so at a later time by the lack of appropriate credits. This issue is analyzed in more detail in Chapter 5.

There were few differences between minority group students and white students regarding future vocational plans. As one would expect, more female students than male students aspired to a teacher or therapist role (29 percent of all female students checked this response, against only 13 percent of the male students). Among males, 13 percent of the Oriental-Americans and 11 percent of the Spanish-surname Americans indicated that they hoped to become

---

[2] The occupationally oriented and college transfer-oriented students were identified by sorting all students responding to #4, "What is the highest level of education you expect to complete?" into three groups. Those who indicated that they expected to stop with a junior college degree or less (response codes 0 and 1) were classified as "career program" students, those who said they hoped to achieve a bachelor's degree or above (response codes 2 to 8) were grouped as "college transfer" students, and those who responded "other" were labeled "unknown."

TABLE 2.5 Expected level of educational achievement by race and sex (in percentages)

Highest expected level of educ. achievement	Afro-American		Mexican/Spanish-Am.		Caucasian		American Indian		Oriental-American	
	M	F	M	F	M	F	M	F	M	F
Less than 2 years	4	8	3	9	3	5	2	9	1	7
A.A. degree	11	26	7	19	14	25	9	29	21	17
B.A. degree	38	32	34	36	37	36	28	24	27	42
M.A. or M.B.A.	27	22	33	24	26	24	26	23	28	25
Ph.D. Ed.D.	6	5	9	5	7	4	20	6	4	2
M.D. or LL.B.	8	2	11	2	9	1	13	2	14	3
Other	6	4	2	4	4	4	2	7	5	3
Total	100	99	99	99	100	99	100	100	100	99
(Weighted N in thousands)	(134.6)	(81.6)	(28.5)	(16.4)	(357.9)	(305.9)	(9.2)	(7.4)	(8.3)	(5.6)

TABLE 2.6 *Type of program by race and sex (in percentages)*

Type of program	Afro-American		Mexican/Spanish-Am.		Caucasian		American Indian		Oriental-American		Total	
	M	F	M	F	M	F	M	F	M	F	M	F
Career program	17	39	11	30	18	33	11	41	23	25	17	35
College transfer	83	61	89	70	82	67	89	59	77	75	83	65
Total	100	100	100	100	100	100	100	100	100	100	100	100
(Weighted N in thousands)	(128.9)	(83.7)	(28.2)	(15.9)	(350.1)	(302.1)	(9.0)	(6.9)	(7.9)	(5.5)	(553.2)	(447.9)

researchers or investigators, compared with only 2 percent of their female counterparts.

Among ethnic groups, the overall level of satisfaction with their college experience varied (see Table 2.7). Students of Oriental or American Indian extraction, particularly the male students, indicated that it was a less than satisfactory experience. Of the males, 37 percent of the American Indian students and 47 percent of the Oriental students responding to the question on overall satisfaction indicated that they were indifferent to or dissatisfied with that experience. Since both of these minority groups have only recently begun to agitate for greater recognition, their persisting frustrations may be reflected in these findings. Male American Indian students found high school inadequate (see Table 2.8), while the remaining ethnic groups viewed high school as good to excellent (approximately 46 percent of the black, Spanish-surname, Oriental, and white students rated high school in this manner). Female students rated both college and high school as more satisfying than did male students.

Age, Sex, Marital Status

Full-time students at community and junior colleges were older than their four-year college peers. Of the entering freshmen participating in the Project Focus survey, 25 percent reported that they were 21 years of age or over, while only 7 percent reported this in 1967 (see Table 2.9). While the age distribution in the four-year institutions has continued to fall predominantly in the 18- to 20-year-old bracket, the enrollment of older students in the two-year colleges has risen steadily. Female students fell into a bimodal distribution, with 29 percent in the 18 and under age group and 8 percent in the 30 and over group (see Table 2.10). Male students were more normally distributed, with 19 percent in the 18 and under age group, 45 percent in the 19 to 20 age group, 24 percent in the 21 to 24 age group, and 12 percent in the 25 years of age and over category. Since the Project Focus data included only full-time students, the median age here (20 years) is well below the median age of the total student body, both full- and part-time students, as part-time students were reported elsewhere as having a median age of 27 years. [30, p. 70]

The older the student, the more likely it is that he will find his college experience satisfying. Table 2.11 reveals a consistent trend toward increased satisfaction as the age of the student increases. Note that the older the junior college student, the more polarized he

TABLE 2.7   *Level of satisfaction with college by race and sex (in percentages)*

Level of satisfaction	Afro-American		Mexican/Spanish-Am.		Caucasian		American Indian		Oriental-American	
	M	F	M	F	M	F	M	F	M	F
Completely satis. & satis.	66	71	72	75	72	76	63	77	53	64
Indifferent	21	19	15	17	18	13	21	9	35	20
Unsatis. & completely unsatis.	13	10	13	8	11	11	16	15	12	17
Total	100	100	100	100	101	100	100	100	100	101
(Weighted N in thousands)	(136.1)	(85.5)	(28.4)	(16.5)	(359.5)	(311.4)	(9.2)	(7.4)	(8.3)	(5.6)

TABLE 2.8   Adequacy of high school education by race and sex (in percentages)

Adequacy of high school	Afro-American		Mexican/ Spanish-Am.		Caucasian		American Indian		Oriental-American	
	M	F	M	F	M	F	M	F	M	F
Excellent to good	39	51	45	55	48	58	36	49	41	58
Average	43	47	34	34	38	33	41	35	50	33
Below average to very inadequate	18	12	21	11	15	9	23	16	8	9
Total	100	100	100	100	101	100	100	100	99	100
(Weighted N in thousands)	(135.9)	(84.7)	(28.6)	(16.3)	(359.3)	(310.8)	(9.2)	(7.4)	(8.3)	(5.6)

TABLE 2.9   Ages of entering freshmen in two- and four-year college programs
by year of enrollment (in percentages)

	1967*		1970*		1971	
Age	2 Yr.	4 Yr.	2 Yr.	4 Yr.	2 Yr.†	4 Yr.*
17 & under	2	6	3	4	2	4
18-20	91	92	83	94	74	94
21 & over	7	2	15	2	25	2
Total	100	100	101	100	101	100

*Data taken from the American Council on Education's *The American Freshman: National Norms.*
†Data obtained from Project Focus survey.

becomes in his views of college. The percentage reporting that they are unsatisfied or completely unsatisfied remains relatively constant with age, however. It seems logical that the longer a student has to wait to obtain a college education, the higher the value he will place on it.

Approximately 80 percent of the students attending community junior colleges full time are single. Of those that are married, 83 percent are 21 years old and over (see Table 2.12). Of the married women, 64 percent are 25 years of age or over. Many of these women are resuming their formal education after their offspring have reached school age.

Four times as many married students as single students identify

TABLE 2.10   Age distribution by year in college and sex (in percentages)

	Freshman		Sophomore		Total	
Age	M	F	M	F	M	F
17 & under	1	2	0	0	1	2
18	28	39	2	3	18	27
19-20	41	41	55	69	46	50
21-24	20	7	28	12	23	9
25-29	6	4	10	6	8	5
30 & over	4	7	5	10	4	8
Total	100	100	100	100	100	101
(Weighted N in thousands)	(384.4)	(321.0)	(249.4)	(169.3)	(633.8)	(490.3)

TABLE 2.11 Level of satisfaction with college by age and sex (in percentages)

Level of satisfaction	18 & Under		19-20		21-24		25 & Over	
	M	F	M	F	M	F	M	F
Completely satis. & satis.	67	72	68	72	73	80	76	89
Indifferent	21	17	20	16	17	11	15	5
Unsatis. & completely unsatis.	12	11	12	12	11	10	9	6
Total	100	100	100	100	101	101	100	100
(Weighted N in thousands)	(115.3)	(139.3)	(292.1)	(246.3)	(146.9)	(41.6)	(76.6)	(61.1)

TABLE 2.12   *Marital status by age and sex (in percentages)*

	Single		Married	
Age	*M*	*F*	*M*	*F*
18 & under	23	32	4	4
19-20	54	59	10	17
21-24	20	7	43	15
25 & over	3	2	43	64
Total	100	100	100	100
(Weighted N in thousands)	(504.2)	(396.2)	(102.4)	(64.5)

the GI bill or veterans benefits as their principal source of income
(see Table 2.13). Almost half of the single students consider their
parents a primary source of support, while 26 percent of the married
students depend primarily on spouses. Separated, divorced, and
widowed students are more apt to depend upon loans, EOG grants,
and work-study programs as their principal source of income.

Student Socioeconomic Background

Since students are the product of their sociocultural experiences,
these factors need to be understood if appropriate learning experi-

TABLE 2.13   *Marital status by principal source of financial support (in percentages)*

Source of income	*Single*	*Married*	*Separated, divorced, or widowed*
Parents	46	8	10
Spouse	1	26	4
Employment or savings	26	19	26
Loans or EOG	10	7	21
G.I. Bill or veterans benefits	8	34	26
Scholarship or grant	7	3	4
Other	2	3	9
Total	100	100	100
(Weighted N in thousands)	(898.5)	(165.8)	(29.8)

ences are to be designed with motivation and study habits in mind. Such factors as father's occupation, parental education attainment, and family income have been employed as indirect measures of a family's social-class position.

One of the more important determinants of socioeconomic status is the occupational role of the head of the household. Since 75 percent or more of the respondents indicate that both parents are alive and still married, the head of household is assumed to be the father. Table 2.14 presents the occupational role of fathers broken out by the race and sex of the full-time community junior college student. Skilled and semiskilled tradesmen are mentioned most frequently; about one out of three students indicates this as their fathers' occupation. Managerial or executive is the next most frequent occupation listed, with about one out of six students identifying this as their fathers' occupation. Eight percent of the students list their fathers' occupation as professional, while six percent indicate semiprofessional or technical-level occupations. Small business owner or farm owner is indicated by 14 percent of the students as their fathers' principal occupation, and 9 to 10 percent identify their fathers as supervisors or public officials. A little over 8 percent of the student body list their fathers' occupation as unskilled, and the remaining 6 percent of the students list their fathers as salesmen. When the responses are broken down by ethnic background, black, Spanish-surname, and American Indian students report a higher percentage of fathers working as unskilled laborers. In general, the occupational background of the fathers of white students is skewed towards the upper end of the occupational structure, while the reverse is true for those from minority group backgrounds. The data, when viewed from the perspective of the democratizing effect of community junior colleges, demonstrate that students from lower socioeconomic backgrounds are able to continue their education because of the availability of a community junior college.

There is some tendency for a student enrolled in the college transfer program to have come from a family where the fathers' occupation was managerial or executive. About two out of four students in the college transfer program come from such families, compared with only 17 percent of the career-oriented A.A. degree students. Two out of every five career-oriented students have fathers who were either skilled or semiskilled workers, against three out of ten in the college transfer program.

There are few differences between students from white-collar

TABLE 2.14　Father's occupation by race and sex (in percentages)

Occupation	Afro-American		Mexican/ Spanish-Am.		Caucasian		American Indian		Oriental-American		Total	
	M	F	M	F	M	F	M	F	M	F	M	F
Manager or executive	15	12	12	9	16	19	31	10	3	18	16	17
Prof.	7	8	5	3	9	8	10	1	9	5	8	8
Semiprof. or tech.	6	4	6	1	6	6	2	6	10	7	6	6
Supr. or pub. off.	8	8	8	5	11	10	7	6	8	9	10	9
Sm. busi. or farm owner	12	11	13	13	16	15	12	12	28	31	15	14
Sales	8	6	4	8	6	7	7	9	1	2	6	7
Skilled or semiskill.	33	34	31	38	31	30	20	44	36	19	31	31
Unskilled	11	17	21	22	6	6	11	13	5	9	8	9
Total	100	100	100	99	101	101	100	101	100	99	100	101
(Weighted N in thousands)	(131.1)	(78.5)	(27.7)	(15.6)	(346.7)	(299.8)	(9.1)	(6.8)	(8.2)	(5.1)	(522.8)	(405.8)

backgrounds and those from blue-collar backgrounds in terms of expected income ten years after graduation. There is, however, a slight upward skewing of expected incomes among the students from managerial, executive, or professional backgrounds. Among the male students, for example, 50 percent of those with a managerial, executive, or professional family background expect to be earning over $15,000 a year in ten years. In contrast, only 35 percent of those listing their fathers as semiskilled or unskilled workers state that they expect an income of $15,000 or more a year in the next ten years.

A somewhat similar situation appears when the father's occupational status is compared with the student's expected level of educational attainment. Of students from managerial, executive, and professional backgrounds, 16 percent anticipate receiving a Ph.D., M.D., or LL.B., while only 9 percent of those from semiskilled or unskilled family backgrounds have similar aspirations. All in all, the occupational status of fathers does not make a significant difference in students' levels of aspiration. The fact of college enrollment seems to have an equalizing effect on student aspirations.

Cross-tabulating the educational level of the father with the student's own educational aspirations again reveals little correlation between a student's socioeconomic status and his educational aspirations. Approximately 36 percent of all students aspire to a B.A. degree, whether the father has less than a high school education or is a college graduate. Approximately one out of five students hope to achieve an A.A. degree, and about 35 percent of the students aspire to a graduate degree. This suggests that even first-generation college students (first in their families) have learned to aspire to as high an educational level as possible, regardless of their socioeconomic background.

In addition to the head of household's occupation and educational attainment level, estimated family income can also serve as an index of socioeconomic status. To avoid any confusion about "family income," the student was asked to indicate his parents' income before taxes. Our earlier analysis revealed that the overall distribution of parental incomes matched that for the United States as a whole. For purposes of this analysis, students were grouped into three income categories—low, medium, and high—to facilitate cross-tabulations. All parental income below $5,000 was designated as the low-income category, $5,000 to 14,999 was rated as medium, and $15,000 and above was high. The low-income bracket included 7 percent of all students, 37 percent identified themselves as in the middle range, and 33 percent were in the high-parental-income bracket. Twenty-two percent of the students indicated they did not know, or considered this information confidential. Slightly more than half (52 percent) of the low-income students were female, while three out of five (60 percent) in the middle and high categories were male.

When parental income is cross-tabulated with the student's principal source of income, the results show that the low-income student depends much more upon loans and EOG grants as his principal source of income than does the high-parental-income student. Of male students falling into the low-parental-income bracket, 25 percent identify the GI bill or veterans benefits as their principal source of income, while only 16 percent of the high-parental-income students do so (see Table 2.15). Parents, spouses, and employment or savings are identified as principal sources of income by 72 percent of the high-parental-income male students, compared to 52 percent of the low-parental-income male students. It is reasonable to expect that more of the low-income students would have relied on NDEA loans, EOG grants, and scholarship aid had these been available to them. Our interviews revealed, however, that because such students are often the last to apply, a large proportion of the money available is often already allocated. The distribution and utilization of federally sponsored student aid programs needs further evaluation before a definitive statement can be made concerning its utilization by low-income students.

Surprisingly, the percentage of low-income students enrolled in private junior colleges is higher than that for the public community colleges. Table 2.16 reveals that 15 percent of private junior college students and only 9 percent of the public community college students fall into the low-income bracket. The reliability of these findings may be open to question, however, because of the relatively small sample and the large number (30 percent) of private junior college students who either did not know their parents' income or did not want to provide that information.

As one might expect, the lower-income students come from families where the father was either semiskilled or unskilled. Also, low-income students are much more likely to have fathers whose educational attainment level is less than high school.

Low-income students expect the same income level ten years from now as do higher-income students. About one out of three students from both the low- and high-parental-income categories expect to earn $15,000 or more per year ten years after graduation. This finding reinforces our earlier observation that students from low-

TABLE 2.15 Family income level by primary source of financial support by sex (in percentages)

| Level of family income* | Primary source of financial support | | | | | | | | | | | | | (Weighted N in thousands) | |
| | Parents or spouse | | Employment or savings | | Loan or EOG | | G.I. bill | | Scholarship or grant | | Other | | Total | | | |
	M	F	M	F	M	F	M	F	M	F	M	F	M	F	M	F
Low	29	51	22	18	13	18	25	4	6	6	4	4	100	101	(38.2)	(38.7)
Medium	29	40	31	24	11	18	20	6	7	10	2	2	100	100	(251.6)	(167.4)
High	42	60	30	21	6	9	16	4	3	5	2	2	99	101	(226.9)	(148.9)

TABLE 2.16 Family income level by type of institutional governance (in percentages)

Level of family income*	Public	Private	Total
Low	9	15	10
Medium	48	41	48
High	43	44	43
Total	100	100	101
(Weighted N in thousands)	(812.3)	(69.5)	(881.8)

*Respondents who did not know their parents' income or who did not want to provide the information have been eliminated from this table.

income backgrounds who manage to enroll in college share the same aspirations as those from middle- or higher-income brackets. The same observation holds true for educational aspirations—as many low-income as high-income students expect to go on to a master's degree or other graduate-level training before completing their formal education. Whether the low-income students come to college because of their upwardly mobile aspirations or acquire them after enrollment cannot, of course, be determined from the data. It is appropriate to observe, however, that a community or junior college experience does seem to raise the aspiration levels of the disadvantaged and the minority student.

FACULTY CHARACTERISTICS

Having completed our analysis of the characteristics, aspirations, and attitudes of students, we are now in a position to evaluate the qualifications of the community junior college faculty and their ability to accomodate such a diverse array of student interests and needs. Not a great deal is known about the two-year college faculty member other than normative data on degrees earned, salary status, and previous work experience. How satisfied faculty members are with their work and how they see themselves in comparison with faculty members of other institutions of higher education has been the focus of a number of studies. [29] What training they have received and the value of that experience has been a point of contention between critics and supporters of two-year colleges for years. Their previous experience, aspirations, and attitudes about their work will serve as the focus of our discussion for the remainder of the chapter.

First, a brief note concerning the survey instrument. Limited dollar resources made it necessary to restrict the questionnaire administered to a representative cross section of faculty to a preprinted optical scan answer sheet. This in turn restricted the number of questions and the range of responses available to the respondents. Key demographic data such as questions on age and socioeconomic status had to be left out. What follows is a synthesis of information taken from two or three recent studies, including, of course, the findings from the Project Focus investigation.

The full-time community junior college teaching staff is predominantly white and male. Women constitute less than 30 percent of the full-time faculty. Ninety-two percent of the faculty are white, with the remainder equally distributed among blacks, American

Indians, Mexican or Spanish-speaking Americans, and Oriental-Americans (see Table 2.24). The lack of representation of minorities on the faculty, in spite of a greatly expanded enrollment of minority students recently, should be, and is, a cause for concern.

According to a recently published study conducted by the Bureau of Social Science Research, [30, p. 206] 55 percent of the full-time faculty of public community colleges came from families where fathers were employed in either professional, managerial, clerical, or sales positions. Only 35 percent were from blue-collar backgrounds. Interestingly enough, in the same study, fewer than one-fifth of the full-time faculty reported fathers with a college or graduate degree. Approximately 43 percent reported that their fathers had less than a high school diploma. More female than male full-time faculty members reported fathers with college degrees.

Two-year college faculty members are predominantly nonurban in background. [30, p. 209] Approximately 40 percent grew up in a rural or small-town environment. One-third came from a truly urban setting, having lived in cities larger than 100,000.

These background characteristics, with the significant exception of ethnic status, demonstrate that the full-time faculty members of community junior colleges come from backgrounds comparable to those of the students whom they teach. Such backgrounds could be described as lower middle class, nonurban, and semiprofessional. How well the upwardly mobile faculty member accepts students of comparable or lower socioeconomic status is open to question, as is the ability of such teachers to empathize with their students. Add to this the observation that most faculty members have had a limited exposure to situations outside the academic world and the problem is further compounded. While it is dangerous to make sweeping generalizations, one obvious conclusion is that many of those trained and employed as teachers in community junior colleges have credentials acquired in a university environment, which is geared to a different kind of student.

Occupational Qualifications and Experience

Full-time faculty at community junior colleges are a relatively inexperienced group. Almost one-third have been teaching for five years or less. Those who teach liberal arts courses are slightly more experienced than those in occupational programs (see Table 2.17).[3]

[3] Faculty members were classified as "academic" or "occupational" according to their departmental affiliation. Those rated as "unclassified" failed to indicate their departmental status.

TABLE 2.17   Years taught by academic-occupational orientation—full-time
faculty (in percentages)

Years	Academic	Occupational	Unclassified	Total
1-5	28.9	44.0	17.2	31.9
6-10	29.2	26.5	29.5	28.6
11-15	19.2	12.0	23.0	17.7
16-20	9.1	7.6	13.4	8.9
21-25	6.2	5.5	5.7	6.0
26-30	2.9	1.5	5.4	2.7
31-35	3.1	1.7	2.3	2.8
36+	1.3	1.2	3.5	1.4
Total	100.0	100.0	100.0	100.0
(Weighted N in thousands)	(48.5)	(15.5)	(2.6)	(66.6)

Of the liberal arts or academic faculty, 43 percent indicated that
they had eleven or more years of teaching experience, while only 33
percent of the occupational faculty indicated this.

Of those who were employed in other educational institutions
before accepting their present appointment, 38 percent were
employed in a high school, 11 percent worked in an elementary or
junior high school, and 27 percent served as faculty members of a
four-year college or university. These findings compare favorably
with the backgrounds reported by Medsker and Tillery [49] and
Godfrey and Holmstrom. [30] As might be expected, one-fifth of
the occupational faculty had previously worked in a vocational high
school or technical institute, while only 3 percent of the liberal arts
faculty had done so (see Table 2.18). Godfrey and Holmstrom [30,
p. 231] found that only 15 percent decided to become two-year
college instructors after starting another career.

Three out of four community junior college faculty members have
a master's degree. Five percent have completed a Ph.D. or Ed.D.
Table 2.19 compares the academic and occupational faculty in terms
of highest degree held. Among the academic faculty, 90 percent have
a master's degree or higher, while only 52 percent of the occupational faculty have reached this educational level. Many of the
occupational faculty chose education as their profession after
spending a number of years in another field, presumably one related
to their area of specialization. However, the gap between the
education level of occupational instructors and of those in the

TABLE 2.18   Previous employment by academic-occupational orientation—
full-time faculty (in percentages)

Type of school	Academic	Occupational	Unclassified	Total
Elementary-junior high school	12.3	4.1	12.7	10.7
High school	40.4	30.0	29.1	37.9
Vocational, technical high school	1.7	7.6	3.1	2.9
Technical institute	1.5	10.9	1.5	3.3
Junior-community college	10.4	11.5	13.8	10.8
Four-year college, university	28.5	21.1	21.9	26.8
Other	5.2	14.8	17.9	7.6
Total	100.0	100.0	100.0	100.0
(Weighted N in thousands)	(35.3)	(8.8)	(2.0)	(46.1)*

*The large block of nonrespondents (approximately 32 percent) is due to those who had not taught elsewhere or failed to respond to the question.

academic field is being reduced, as almost half of the occupational faculty are currently enrolled in an advanced degree training program (see Table 2.20). One out of three of the liberal arts faculty are similarly enrolled. Six percent of those seeking advanced degrees are working towards their Ph.D. or Ed.D.

TABLE 2.19   Highest degree held by academic-occupational orientation—
full-time faculty (in percentages)

Degree	Academic	Occupational	Unclassified	Total
High school	0.7	11.6	5.4	3.4
A.A., A.A.S., A.S.	0.6	6.9	4.2	2.2
B.A., B.S., B.Ed.	9.2	29.4	10.3	13.9
M.A., M.S., M.Ed.	82.6	51.6	71.7	75.0
Ph.D., Ed.D.	6.9	0.5	8.4	5.5
Total	100.0	100.0	100.0	100.0
(Weighted N in thousands)	(48.5)	(15.3)	(2.6)	(66.4)

TABLE 2.20   Degree presently sought by academic-occupational orientation—
full-time faculty (in percentages)

Degree	Academic	Occupational	Unclassified	Total
High school	1.7	2.2	13.1	2.4
A.A., A.A.S., A.S.	0.5	3.9	2.6	1.5
B.A., B.S., B.Ed.	1.9	19.6	2.6	6.7
M.A., M.S., M.Ed.	21.7	49.7	19.1	29.1
Ph.D., Ed.D.	74.2	24.6	62.6	60.3
Total	100.0	100.0	100.0	100.0
(Weighted N in thousands)	(16.1)	(6.4)	(1.2)	(23.6)*

*Nonrespondents presumably are those not enrolled in a degree-oriented
program.

One might well ask how appropriate this form of additional
graduate study is for those planning to teach at a community junior
college. Teachers who are confronted with a heterogeneous population of students, many from unfamiliar cultural backgrounds, might
better spend their time studying the ethnic heritage and cultural
environment of the students they teach. Learning to prepare course
objectives or to construct performance tests, while important, does
not necessarily help the instructor empathize with his students or
help them achieve higher levels of self-confidence. Unfortunately,
many graduate school programs follow the traditional university
pedagogy and are not geared to the unique functions of the
community junior college.

Dr. Roger Garrison of Westbrook College in Maine, in his seminal
study of the community junior college faculty, [29, p. 15] made the
following observations concerning teachers at two-year postsecondary institutions:

Markedly different . . . are his conditions of institutions, his aims, and his
professional philosophical attitudes toward his task. Not simply a post-high
school instructor of grades thirteen and fourteen, he is, in his own view, a
colleague in a new kind of collegiate effort, as yet ill-defined and in furious flux.
He is unsure of his status in the educational spectrum, for he fits few traditional
categories. He is aware that he is being asked to function professionally in an
unprecedented situation, and he is deeply concerned about his professionalism,
in the best sense of that term.

The proliferation of new two-year colleges during the past decade has created a new market for instructors who are neither research-oriented nor necessarily committed to a single academic discipline. Despite the pronouncements of some authorities, most two-year college administrators are not seeking recent Ph.D.s steeped in the tradition of graduate research. First, and foremost, they want capable teachers. Community junior college instructors must be able to understand and meet the needs of a locally based constituency, some of whom are disadvantaged, some of whom are older, and many of whom are part-time students. They must be able to relate to, empathize with, and reinforce such students. Unfortunately, most Ph.D.s are not trained to do any of these things. This is not the place to offer suggestions for improving the preservice training of community junior college instructors; it is sufficient to observe that the present training program for those about to enter the portals of two-year colleges needs overhauling. More will be offered on this point in Chapter 5.

Career Aspirations

When asked to indicate where they expected to be five years from now, 80 percent of those who expected to remain in education indicated that they hoped to be teaching in a community or junior college (see Table 2.21), while 14 percent hoped to move on to a four-year college or university. Of those who predicted that they would not be in education in five years, 37 percent expected to retire and the remainder listed such goals as marriage, employment in private industry, or self-employment. It should be noted that only 10 percent of the total population of full-time faculty predicted that they would no longer be actively involved in education five years hence (see Table 2.22).

Certain differences appear when the academically and occupationally oriented faculty are compared on this subject. Of those who predict that they will not be affiliated with an educational institution, almost half of the academic faculty expect to retire, while only 18 percent of the occupationally oriented faculty will do so. On the other hand, a larger percentage (31 percent) of the occupational faculty anticipate employment in private industry.

Table 2.22 indicates that only 6 percent of the total faculty group were thinking of leaving education for another type of occupation. This finding closely parallels that of the Godfrey-Holmstrom study. [30, p. 189] The few that want to change jobs yet remain

TABLE 2.21   Expected employment five years from now by academic-occupational orientation—full-time faculty (in percentages)

Employment	Academic	Occupational	Unclassified	Total
Educationally oriented:				
High school	0.3	0.3	. . .	0.3
Vocational-technical institute	1.9	9.4	3.0	3.5
Junior-community college	80.5	79.2	82.7	80.3
Four-year college, university	15.4	9.6	13.3	14.1
Other	1.9	1.5	1.0	1.8
Total	100.0	100.0	100.0	100.0
(Weighted N in thousands)	(42.4)	(11.9)	(2.0)	(56.2)
Noneducationally oriented:	*Academic*	*Occupation*	*Unclassified*	*Total*
Marriage	9.3	18.5	5.1	13.0
Private industry	9.8	30.7	8.3	16.2
Government	2.5	3.5	. . .	2.6
Self-employed	16.2	9.3	13.8	14.8
Retired	48.7	18.5	19.4	37.1
Other	3.7	4.9	8.3	4.3
Undecided	9.8	14.6	5.1	12.0
Total	100.0	100.0	100.0	100.0
(Weighted N in thousands)	(4.1)	(2.1)	(0.4)	(6.6)

within the field of education indicate that they expect to move on to a four-year college or university.

While the numbers are small, and should therefore be interpreted with caution, a larger proportion of the occupational faculty expects to change from the role of educator to something else. This is understandable when we realize that the occupational instructor teaches more hours than his academic counterpart and is paid less. He is more likely to be Caucasian and, as we saw earlier, is not as well trained as the academic instructor (in terms of degrees earned) (see

TABLE 2.22   Expected employment five years from now by highest degree obtained—full-time faculty (in percentages)

Expected employment	Highest degree obtained				
	A.A. degree	B.A. degree	M.A. degree	Ph.D. or Ed.D.	Total
Educationally oriented:					
Community-junior col.	56	64	76	57	73
Vocational-technical center	14	10	1	. . .	2
College or university	2	9	13	24	13
Other	2	1	2	8	2
Noneducationally oriented:					
Retirement	2	1	4	7	4
Business and industry	20	9	2	2	3
Undecided or other	5	6	2	2	3
Total	101	100	100	100	100
(Weighted N in thousands)	(1.15)	(8.12)	(47.1)	(3.33)	(59.7)

Tables 2.23 and 2.24). We can only hypothesize that minority faculty members are not as likely to teach occupational courses because such opportunities were only recently opened to them. Those who did achieve graduate degrees were channeled or chose to go into the traditional academic disciplines.

Breaking the faculty population down by highest degree held against future plans, those with higher degrees are more likely not only to remain in education but to want to continue working in a community junior college. Of those holding an A.A. degree, 20 percent expect to be working elsewhere, while only 4 percent of those with an M.A. degree or above expect to do so. However, 24 percent of those with Ph.D.s hope to move on to a four-year college or university, thereby confirming the suspicion that some of this group view the two-year college as a way station in their career.

TABLE 2.23   Class hours spent in actual student instruction by academic-occupational orientation—full-time faculty (in percentages)

Number of hours	Academic	Occupational	Unclassified	Total
0-10	15.0	9.6	48.9	15.3
11-15	45.5	25.1	20.9	39.6
16-20	23.5	29.6	16.0	24.6
21+	16.0	35.7	14.2	20.5
Total	100.0	100.0	100.0	100.0
(Weighted N in thousands)	(48.7)	(15.6)	(2.8)	(67.2)

Faculty Attitudes toward Work

The overall level of work satisfaction among full-time faculty in community junior colleges is high. Complete satisfaction or satisfaction with their college was indicated by 91 percent, while only 5 percent responded at the opposite end of the scale; 3½ percent stated that they were indifferent. There was essentially no difference between the level of satisfaction of the academic faculty and that of

TABLE 2.24   Full-time faculty minority group status by academic-occupational orientation (in percentages)

Ethnic status	Academic	Occupational	Unclassified	Total
Nonminority				
Caucasian/white	92.0	93.5	83.8	92.1
Minority				
Afro-American/ black	1.7	0.9	1.3	1.5
American Indian	1.1	0.3	3.4	1.0
Mexican/Spanish-American	1.4	0.8	5.5	1.4
Oriental-Amer.	0.8	1.6	2.1	1.0
Other	1.3	1.2	1.3	1.3
Not responding	1.7	1.6	2.5	1.7
Total	100.0	100.0	100.0	100.0
(Weighted N in thousands)	(48.4)	(15.5)	(2.4)	(66.3)

the occupational faculty, although a slightly higher percentage of the academic group indicated complete satisfaction (20 percent as against 15 percent of the occupational faculty members).

When asked which of the following aspects of their job they disliked most, 16 percent of the respondents indicated that they did not have enough time to prepare adequately for their classes or to keep themselves up to date. (Approximately one-third felt there were no drawbacks in their present role.) Among those teaching in private junior colleges, 20 percent complained that the biggest drawback of their job was working with unappreciative or unmotivated students. Only 10 percent of the public community college instructors responded in a like manner. It is apparent from these findings that most faculty members find few drawbacks with their work.

Most community junior college faculty members feel that they have a harder job than their counterparts in the four-year colleges. Sixty-three percent of the respondents indicated that they agreed with this statement. In terms of job importance compared to faculty members of four-year institutions, slightly more than 60 percent of the community junior college faculty agreed that their work was more important. Again, there was essentially no difference between the academic and the occupational faculty.

Over the last decade, a number of researchers [54] have expressed concern over whether or not two-year college faculty members strongly endorse the stated purposes of their institutions. Our data, while not definitive, support Medsker's observation [48] that some faculty members identify more closely with the faculties of four-year institutions than they do with their own colleagues. Almost a third of the survey respondents felt that community junior colleges should screen students more than they do at present. Additional analysis of faculty support for selected goals of the two-year colleges, presented in a later chapter, also demonstrates that many faculty members do not fully endorse the concept of the open door. The position is understandable when one realizes that the responsibility for educating a mixture of low-achieving or underachieving students and more able students falls squarely on the shoulders of the faculty. The open door is, nevertheless, one of the major tenets of the community college program. Faculty members who are unable, or do not want, to accept this responsibility probably ought to seek work in more compatible settings. Unfortunately, the brevity of the questionnaire did not permit more of an in-depth examination of the rewards and frustrations which the faculty at two-year postsecondary institutions experience in their work. This clearly is a topic worthy of further investigation.

CONTRASTING PERCEPTIONS OF STUDENTS AND
FACULTY

Both students and faculty participating in the survey were asked to
respond to a series of questions dealing with college policies,
practices, facilities, and services. The respondents were asked to rate
the policies, practices, or facilities at their institutions on the basis of
their agreement, partial agreement, or disagreement with the statement posed. They were also asked to rate student services in terms of
whether or not the service was found to be extremely valuable,
worthwhile, of little benefit, or never used. Tables 2.25 and 2.26
summarize the findings.

More faculty than students felt that the rules governing the
invitation of controversial speakers are reasonable. More students
than faculty, on the other hand, felt that adequate provisions are
being made for gifted students.[4] Both faculty and students agree that
instructors are generally available for assistance with classwork when
needed. Examinations are jointly perceived as fair, with approximately 50 percent of both students and faculty agreeing on this
point.

Regarding who has the right to participate in college policy
making, more faculty than students felt that students do have ample
opportunity to participate. Three-fourths of the faculty and a little
over half of the students agree or partly agree with this statement.
One out of four students, however, had no opinion on the matter.
This lack of interest is somewhat surprising when one considers the
number of protests mounted by students in support of their interest
in a larger role in policy making. The next chapter will explore this
issue in greater depth. What is significant here, however, is the fact
that a number of two-year college students do not have strongly held
views on the matter.

The type of college services available to students often determines
the extent to which students are willing or able to continue their
enrollment in college. A common viewpoint, as, for example, both
students and faculty perceiving a particular service as valuable, provides a means of evaluating just how useful a given service is. It must
be recognized that the findings presented here are intracollege. Individual institutional differences will be disguised or muted in the

[4] The high number of "no opinion on the matter" replies made by students reflects their
lack of interest or awareness of their institution's position on this issue. Two-thirds of the
faculty either partly disagree or completely disagree with the institutional policy on this
matter.

TABLE 2.25 Student and faculty perceptions of college policies, practices, and facilities (in percentages)

Nature of college policies, practices, and facilities	Student or faculty perceptions	Agree	Partly agree or disagree	Disagree	No opinion	Total
Rules governing the invitation of controversial speakers are reasonable	S	37	23	12	28	100
	F	57	15	6	22	100
Regulations governing academic probation and dismissal are sensible	S	50	21	11	18	100
	F	61	24	10	5	100
Examinations are usually thorough and fair	S	46	39	11	4	100
	F	52	31	5	12	100
Instructors are generally available for assistance with classwork	S	67	23	6	4	100
	F	69	22	5	4	100
Adequate provision is made for gifted students (e.g., honors programs, independent study, undergraduate research, etc.)	S	28	19	13	40	100
	F	20	36	32	12	100
Students have ample opportunity to participate in college policy making	S	27	29	20	24	100
	F	39	33	18	10	100

TABLE 2.26   Student and faculty perceptions of college services (in percentages)

Type of college service	Student or faculty perceptions	Extremely valuable	Worth-while	Of little benefit	Never used	Not offered or available	Total
Academic advising service (assistance in selecting courses, adjusting schedules, planning programs, etc.)	S	25	38	22	13	2	100
	F	36	48	15	...	1	100
Counseling service (assistance in choosing a major, vocational planning, resolving personal problems, etc.)	S	21	31	22	24	2	100
	F	30	51	17	1	1	100
Orientation service (assistance in getting started in college—learning the ropes, getting acquainted, over coming apprehensions, etc.)	S	16	29	25	24	6	100
	F	23	47	25	1	4	100
Developmental education services (improvement of reading, study skills, spelling, etc.)	S	13	17	9	53	8	100
	F	41	41	7	3	8	100
Financial needs service (assistance in obtaining a scholarship, loan, part-time job; or assistance in budgeting and controlling expenses)	S	19	15	12	51	3	100
	F	48	46	4	1	1	100

process of aggregation. As a nationwide assessment, however, the findings should be of interest.

A little over one-third of the total student population surveyed reported that they found the academic advising service, e.g., assistance in selecting courses, adjusting schedules, planning programs, etc., either of little benefit or never used. However, 84 percent of the faculty rated such a service as worthwhile or extremely valuable. Clearly those responsible for providing this service have not been able to sell a sizable portion of the student body on its benefits.

A similar finding emerges from the rating of the counseling service, e.g., assistance in choosing a major, finding a vocation, resolving personal problems, etc. This service was rated as of little benefit or never used by 46 percent of the students, while 81 percent of the faculty thought it worthwhile or extremely valuable. Such a discrepancy in perceptions puts the counselor squarely on the spot. How such a difference in views can occur at institutions which pride themselves on their emphasis upon student counseling warrants further study. Suffice it to say here that a sizable percentage of students finds this service as it is currently structured to be of little value.

Financial counselors, on the other hand, received better marks for their role in providing information on scholarships, loans, part-time jobs, and advice on budgeting. Of those students who have availed themselves of this service three-fourths found it extremely valuable or worthwhile. A surprisingly large number of students (51 percent), however, stated that they had never consulted a financial aid officer. It seems reasonable to speculate that some portion of this group was not even aware that such a service existed. The remainder, hopefully, did not require such assistance. Of the faculty, 94 percent agreed that this is an extremely valuable or worthwhile program.

Low-income students from minority backgrounds found the financial needs service more valuable than did white students of comparable family income. Of the minority students with family incomes of less than $5,000 a year, 44 percent rated the service as valuable or extremely valuable, while only 31 percent of the low-income white students did so. Even so, 39 percent of the low-income minority students and 54 percent of the low-income whites reported that they never used the service.[5]

[5] Interviews with students revealed that many of those from lower-income families were not aware of the availability of financial counseling until after they enrolled. Those who then sought assistance in the form of grants or loans often discovered that the available monies had already been alloted. For a fuller discussion of this topic, see Gleazer, E. J., Jr., *Project Focus: A Forecast Study of Community Colleges.*

Developmental education programs were seen by the students presumably participating in such programs as worthwhile. Approximately three out of four students benefiting from developmental education programs rated the service as extremely valuable or worthwhile. Slightly over half of the total student group, however, had never been involved. This effort was endorsed by 81 percent of the faculty. Chapter 5 will explore more fully the problems surrounding what is one of the more difficult yet important efforts in the community junior college field. While the data reported here give it reasonably good marks, studies elsewhere have questioned the effectiveness of such programs.

Providing students with assistance in getting started in college, helping them learn the ropes and get acquainted, received a less than enthusiastic rating from both students and faculty. Among the students, 24 percent reported that they never received such assistance, and of those that did, one-third reported that it was of little benefit. Of the faculty, 25 percent agreed with this rating, while slightly less than half thought of it as worthwhile. Looked at from the vantage point of the "new" student, such an orientation (or lack thereof) may well spell the difference between satisfaction with one's experiences in college and a sense of alienation.

From this cursory analysis of student and faculty perceptions of various student service programs, we can conclude that such services leave something to be desired and much to be accomplished. The next chapter will expand this type of intra-institutional comparison and incorporate the viewpoints of the chief executives as well. How students, faculty, and presidents compare on the rank ordering of a selected set of goals and how they weight each goal in terms of desirability and current practice will be its principal message.

Chapter 3.
Institutional Goals and Priorities

Any attempt to compare the long-range goals with the current practices of the nation's community junior colleges must perforce answer the question: What goals are these institutions to serve? This chapter will attempt to provide evidence in support of the observation that, among the 12,800 or so respondents to our goal inventory, there is an emerging consensus on the multiple purposes to be served. Such a consensus among community junior college personnel contrasts dramatically with the agony of debate surrounding the proper role or function of other forms of higher education. Current pressures on the four-year colleges and universities have forced those institutions to take on new roles at a time when their dollar resources are shrinking. While these same pressures are also being felt at the two-year college level, they are being met with a sense of assurance that the right purposes are being pursued.

Students, parents, employers, and politicians no longer accept the statement that four years of postsecondary education is the only sure passport to fame and fortune. Community junior colleges offer an attractive alternative. The public now recognizes that there are a number of well-paying and socially useful occupations that require less than a baccalaureate degree. The high cost and competitiveness of higher education and the growing awareness that continuing educational opportunities are and will be available throughout one's working career—these and other arguments are conspiring to lessen the demand for the traditional four-year degree.

The degree of consensus among the principal participants in community junior colleges on the goals to be served is the primary concern of this chapter. Its major purpose will be to pinpoint similarities and differences in the collective perceptions of students, faculty, and presidents, and to suggest the underlying causes of the differences. Long-range goals and current practices within a particular institution, as perceived by the various groups in the institution, were assessed by means of questionnaires administered to representative samples of students and faculty and to the chief administrator of the institution. Our analysis enabled us to contrast and compare the perceptions of these three groups within institutions of like size (number of students enrolled), age (date organized), and type of governance (public or private).

Students and faculty were drawn at random from the cross-sectional sample of institutions and asked to respond to 12 goal statements taken from the Educational Testing Service's Institutional Goals Inventory (IGI).[1] The presidents of the 90 colleges were asked to respond to a longer list of goal statements, with 12 duplications. Students, faculty, and presidents were asked to rate each goal item in two ways: first, they were asked to rate the items in terms of how much emphasis is being placed on the goal at their institution *at the present time*, and second, the items were to be rated in terms of what the institution's goals *should be during the coming decade*. Each goal statement was to be arrayed on a five-point scale from (1) "emphasized very strongly" down to (5) "emphasized not at all." In terms of what the institution's goals *should be*, the "preferred" goals, they were asked to judge the degree of importance of the goal item on a five-point scale ranging from (1) "of extremely high importance" to (5) "of no importance."

The original intent of ETS was to develop a goal inventory which could be used by colleges and universities to define their goals and establish priorities among them. [65] The staff of Project Focus modified the inventory for specific use in the community junior colleges. Because of time and space limitations in the questionnaires administered to student and faculty groups, only 12 goal statements were utilized. Presidents were asked to respond to 26 goal items in terms of their present and future emphasis.

[1] The items selected for this study were part of a larger instrument developed by the Educational Testing Service (ETS). This modified instrument was adapted and reproduced with their permission. Institutions wishing to administer this inventory will be able to compare mean scores and perceptions obtained with normative data available through ETS.

Mean scores and the rank order of all goal statements were calculated for the three groups of respondents and cross-tabulated for public and private colleges. Relevant institutional characteristics were analyzed to determine the extent to which differences in perception were associated with such characteristics. An index of innovativeness was developed for the purpose of rank-ordering institutions on this dimension, and a limited analysis conducted. Appendix C briefly describes how this instrument was derived. Institutional discrepancy scores were developed to assist presidents and other concerned persons at a given institution in evaluating their own institution's status and made available for use by individual institutions. How each institution might exploit such information in its attempt to achieve a better alignment of their goals and practices will be outlined in the next chapter.

The "goals" [2] of an institution, as distinguished from its "objectives," reflect the broader, longer-term commitments of that institution. Objectives tend to represent more specific and tangible statements which describe the end of an action or represent an intermediate step directed towards a more distant goal. This definition is meant to encompass program objectives, course objectives, student personnel objectives, etc.—the determination of which is primarily the responsibility of the relevant professional responsible for the particular program in question. While goals frequently emerge from the deliberations of concerned groups within an institution, objectives can also be arrived at in a more deliberate

---

[2] Words such as "goal," "function," and "purpose," are often employed interchangeably. For the purposes of this paper, however, the following working definitions are suggested: (1) *Function* will refer to activities that are functionally allied with other social institutions. Such activities are to be viewed in the context of the larger social system. The "cooling out" function, the custodial function, and the certification function represent some of the more noteworthy examples of the "function" of community junior colleges in the larger social order. (2) *Purpose* will be used to describe the mission or collective output of a type of college, e.g., the private, independent college. Such purposes, while politically determined, reflect the collective compromises and adjustments of the institutions in question. The vested interests of those involved in these systems, such as administrators, are often traded off or modified to accomodate the expectations of external groups. (3) *Goals* will refer to the expected outputs and/or priorities of a single college. In the same way that purposes are arrived at for a number of institutions, goals generally emerge as the result of a series of compromises or political accomodations, rather than through a more deliberate or rational process. The greater the number of constituent groups involved, the greater the degree of compromise required. Some institutions enjoy greater autonomy with regard to how priorities in the campus community are treated. Thus the goal definitions of private institutions may reflect a higher degree of rationality than that of public institutions. For a more complete review of the literature on institutional goals, see Richard E. Peterson, *The Crisis of Purpose: Definitions and Uses of Institutional Goals*, ERIC Clearinghouse on Higher Education, Washington, D. C., Report No. 5, 1970.

and rational manner by professionals in the performance of their assigned roles.

"Output" goals, as distinguished from "support" goals, are the collective activities of a given institution as it attempts to carry out its various commitments, e.g., providing higher educational opportunities to all youth from the surrounding community. "Process" goals represent a variety of activities designed to help the organization function in its environment, while at the same time facilitating its achievement of the expected level of "output." [31] The classification of the goal items employed in the study into these two categories is presented in Appendix D.

PRESENT AND FUTURE PRIORITIES

The president of a local institution has the primary responsibility for determining the substance and levels of priority of his institution's goals, but he does so with the advice and consent of others inside and outside the institution. Consequently, the presidents' perceptions of the perceived and preferred goals were considered to be of primary importance. The extent of agreement between a president's perceptions and those of the faculty and students at his institution were also ascertained. By comparing the viewpoints of all three groups, shared expectations and points of tension were highlighted. It was hoped that this information could be used by policymakers within the institutions involved, as well as forming the basis for this national perspective.

Looking at the total sample of institutions, there is a high degree of congruity in the rank-ordering of the same set of goals by presidents and faculty (see Table 3.1). Serving the higher educational needs of youth from the surrounding community, helping students develop a respect for their own abilities and an understanding of their limitations, responding to the needs of the local community, and helping students acquire the ability to adapt to new occupational requirements as technology and society change, all fall into the top third of the desired or preferred goals across institutions as judged or ranked by these two groups.

Presidents tend to emphasize responding to community needs more strongly, while faculty place greater stress on the students' personal development. Note that serving the higher education needs of youth from the local community is rated at or near the top by both groups, indicating a high degree of congruence or support for this output goal.

TABLE 3.1   Presidents' and faculty perceptions of the top six goals for the 70s (rank order of preferred goals)

Presidents	Faculty
1. Serve higher education needs of youth from local community	1. Help students respect own abilities and limitations
2. Respond to needs of local community	2. Serve higher education needs of youth from local community
3. Help students respect own abilities and limitations	3. Help students adapt to new occupational requirements
4. Help students adapt to new occupational requirements	4. Respond to needs of local community
5. Reeducate and retrain those whose vocational capabilities are obsolete	5. Ensure faculty participation in institutional decision making
6. Make financial assistance available to any student who wants to enroll in college	6. Reeducate and retrain those whose vocational capabilities are obsolete

Few dramatic changes occurred when the respondents were asked to rate the various goal items in terms of how much emphasis was *now* being placed on a particular goal. A comparison of the presidents' and faculties' rating of actual goals (in terms of the degree of current emphasis) reveals that only one goal item given a middle-level priority by presidents was given a higher priority by faculty (see Tables 3.2 and 3.3). While the faculty rated "providing some form of education for any student regardless of his academic ability" second on their list of current goals, it fell considerably further down the list among those emphasized by the presidents (fourteenth in rank). Faculty, however, would prefer that this goal receive less attention, moving it from second to seventh position among the preferred goals. It is, of course, the faculty that carries most of the burden of attempting to accommodate the widely varying student needs presented by the open-door college. Faculties are saying that they would like a little less heterogeneity with regard to student backgrounds and abilities and that this current policy needs some modification. The high degree of variance (standard deviation) in both the present and preferred ratings by presidents suggests that there is considerable difference of opinion among presidents regarding their support for this particular goal. The lower

TABLE 3.2   Presidents' ranking of goals*

	Present			Preferred		
	Rank	M	S.D.	Rank	M	S.D.
Serve higher education needs of youth from local community	1	1.39	0.68	2	1.27	0.60
Respond to needs of local community	4	1.81	0.84	6	1.37	0.63
Help students respect own abilities and limitations	6	1.97	0.78	7	1.39	0.56
Help students adapt to new occupational requirements	9	2.13	0.93	9	1.41	0.65
Make financial assistance available to any student who wants to enroll in college	11	2.21	1.07	16	1.74	1.03
Ensure faculty participation in institutional decision making	12	2.22	0.85	19	1.90	0.77
Provide some form of education for any student regardless of academic ability	14	2.36	1.28	18	1.88	1.12
Ensure student participation in institutional decision making	18	2.59	0.92	21	2.18	0.87
Reeducate and retrain those whose vocational capabilities are obsolete	20	2.73	1.10	12	1.62	0.78
Attract representative number of minority faculty members	22	2.92	1.02	24	2.35	0.88
Help formulate programs in public policy areas, e.g., pollution control	24	3.16	1.02	22	2.19	0.93
Allocate percent of enrollment to minority groups or those of low socioeconomic status	25	3.72	1.33	25	3.31	1.36

*Because only 12 goal statements were administered to students and faculty, these same goals were selected from among the 26 rated by presidents for presentation here. Their rank among the 26 has been reported in order that their relative position can be compared with the relative position as rated by faculty and students, i.e., upper, middle, or lower third.

TABLE 3.3 Faculty ranking of goals

	Present			Preferred		
	Rank	M	S.D.	Rank	M	S.D.
Serve higher education needs of youth from local community	1	1.66	0.82	2	1.44	0.67
Provide some form of education for any student regardless of academic ability	2	1.70	0.86	7	1.79	0.96
Respond to needs of local community	3	1.99	0.91	4	1.56	0.71
Help students adapt to new occupational requirements	4	2.12	0.93	3	1.47	0.64
Make financial assistance available to any student who wants to enroll in college	5	2.22	0.94	9	1.88	0.90
Help students respect own abilities and limitations	6	2.24	0.94	1	1.40	0.60
Reeducate and retrain those whose vocational capabilities are obsolete	7	2.41	1.11	6	1.62	0.77
Ensure faculty participation in institutional decision making	8	2.58	1.04	5	1.61	0.73
Ensure student participation in institutional decision making	9	2.85	0.98	10	2.30	0.87
Attract representative number of minority faculty members	10	2.89	1.26	11	2.49	1.06
Help formulate programs in a number of public policy areas, e.g., pollution control	11	2.92	1.11	8	1.86	0.92
Allocate percent of enrollment to minority groups or those of low socioeconomic status	12	3.12	1.35	12	2.81	1.28

the standard deviation, the more confident we are that the rating given a particular goal statement accurately reflects the judgment of the total group involved.

The fact that this goal tends to be ranked lower by both groups under the preferred category than under the perceived or actual practice category suggests that the open-door concept has yet to be fully accepted. Additional comments in a later section of this chapter will reveal some of the differences between institutions in the extent to which this goal is being implemented. Private junior colleges, for example, strive to be more selective than public community colleges—not always successfully, however.

The faculty, as might be expected, evidence less concern with the institutional climate and administrative goals. Their highest-ranked "process" goal is focused on the role of faculty in institutional decision making. They rate it as extremely or quite important. Contrasting this response with their perception of the importance of ensuring student participation in decision making points up one not unexpected difference—that while faculty *are* committed to student development, they are not fully in favor of providing students with an equal voice on matters of policy. Some critics might identify this apparent expression of paternalism as one of the fundamental reasons underlying the rise of student militancy. It should be pointed out, however, that faculty members do feel that this goal is currently being emphasized less than it should be, as reflected in the mean score rating of 2.80 (with 1 being "emphasized very strongly" and 5, "emphasized not at all"). Students, incidentally, give this goal a slightly higher rating on future or preferred importance (2.20) and a slightly lower rating on present emphasis (2.88) than do the faculty (see Table 3.4).

Presidents, however, rank faculty involvement in the lower third of their priorities, with present and preferred mean score ratings of 2.59 and 2.18, respectively. They tend to value the importance of "ensuring faculty participation in decision making" slightly more than "ensuring student participation," but again this goal item falls into the lower third in their ranking of preferred goals. Present emphasis, however, brings it into the middle ranks (from 19 to 12), suggesting that they feel that too much emphasis is currently being given to this policy.

It is apparent from the pattern of responses that the faculty and students feel they are not sufficiently involved in decision making. Presidents, on the other hand, indicate that perhaps both groups are more involved than they should be. Recognizing the lower-ranked status assigned by presidents to this goal relative to the other goal items, in contrast with the responses of students and faculty, one is tempted to conclude that pressure from students and faculty for greater involvement in policy making has been counterbalanced by the reluctance of presidents to yield further on this issue. This apparent state of equilibrium, with students and faculty feeling they should have a little more representation and presidents feeling that

TABLE 3.4   Student ranking of goals

	Present			Preferred		
	Rank	M	S.D.	Rank	M	S.D.
Serve higher education needs of youth from local community	1	2.18	1.04	3	1.77	0.88
Provide some form of education for any student regardless of academic ability	2	2.19	1.08	4	1.85	0.95
Make financial assistance available to any student who wants to enroll in college	3	2.23	1.04	1	1.73	0.90
Help students respect own abilities and limitations	4	2.41	1.04	2	1.76	0.87
Help students adapt to new occupational requirements	5	2.58	1.06	5	1.88	0.87
Ensure faculty participation in institutional decision making	6	2.63	1.04	10	2.18	0.91
Reeducate and retrain those whose vocational capabilities are obsolete	7	2.67	1.14	7	1.95	0.91
Respond to needs of local community	8	2.68	1.10	9	2.10	0.94
Ensure student participation in institutional decision making	9	2.87	1.05	8	2.03	0.90
Allocate per cent of enrollment to minority groups or those of low socioeconomic status	10	2.88	1.14	11	2.36	1.07
Help formulate programs in a number of public policy areas, e.g., pollution control	11	2.95	1.14	6	1.91	0.95
Attract representative number of minority faculty members	12	3.33	1.10	12	2.44	1.02

these groups should have a little less, may well represent the most expedient arrangement at this stage of development.

PRESIDENTS SET THE TONE

The presidents' ranking and rating of 26 goals is presented in Table 3.5. Of the goals which rank among the top third, five are output

TABLE 3.5   Presidents' perceptions of goals for the 70s (N = 90)

	Present			Preferred		
Goal	*Rank*	*Mean*	*S.D.*	*Rank*	*Mean*	*S.D.*
Serve higher education needs of youth from local community	1	1.39	0.68	2	1.27	0.60
Encourage mutal trust and respect among faculty, students, and administrators	2	1.71	0.73	1	1.26	0.47
Establish and define institutional purposes	3	1.81	0.76	3	1.28	0.56
Respond to needs of local community	4	1.81	0.84	6	1.37	0.63
Make financial assistance available to any academically qualified student	5	1.84	0.85	8	1.40	0.63
Help students respect own abilities and limitations	6	1.97	0.78	7	1.39	0.56
Maintain an atmosphere of intellectual excitement on campus	7	2.04	0.90	4	1.35	0.60
Provide educational opportunities for adults in the local area	8	2.11	0.99	10	1.53	0.71
Help students adapt to new occupational requirements	9	2.13	0.93	9	1.41	0.65
Provide wide range of opportunities for specific occupational preparation	10	2.19	1.05	14	1.72	0.93
Make financial assistance available to any student who wants to enroll	11	2.21	1.07	16	1.74	1.03
Ensure faculty participation in institutional decision making	12	2.22	0.85	19	1.90	0.77
Provide for curricular and instructional evaluation	13	2.28	0.80	5	1.36	0.55
Provide some form of education for any student regardless of academic ability	14	2.36	1.28	18	1.88	1.12
Experiment with new forms of instruction	15	2.39	0.79	13	1.70	0.66

TABLE 3.5   Presidents' perceptions of goals for the 70s (N = 90) (continued)

Goal	Present			Preferred		
	Rank	Mean	S.D.	Rank	Mean	S.D.
Increase number and diversity of sources of income	16	2.44	1.15	11	1.57	0.90
Encourage students to undertake self-directed study	17	2.57	1.00	15	1.72	0.75
Ensure student participation in institutional decision making	18	2.59	0.92	21	2.18	0.87
Develop programs for the special student, e.g., disadvantaged, bright, foreign	19	2.63	1.02	17	1.87	0.93
Reeducate and retrain those whose vocational capabilities are obsolete	20	2.73	1.10	12	1.62	0.78
Permit student wide latitude in course selection	21	2.85	0.92	20	21.5	0.90
Attract representative number of minority faculty members	22	2.92	1.02	24	2.35	0.88
Help solve social, economic, or political problems in the immediate geographic area	23	3.09	0.95	23	2.32	1.03
Help formulate programs in a number of public policy areas, e.g., pollution control	24	3.16	1.02	22	2.19	0.93
Allocate percent of enrollment for minority groups or those of low socioeconomic status	25	3.72	1.33	25	3.31	1.36
Strengthen religious faith of students	26	3.80	1.14	26	3.38	1.32

goals and four are process goals. Note that all the higher-ranked perceived goals are also included among the higher-ranked preferred goals, with one exception.

This one exception is providing for curricular and instructional evaluation, fifth among the preferred goals but thirteenth in terms of current emphasis. Presidents recognize that there is considerable room for improvement in this area.

The fact that the majority of top-ranked goals in both the present and preferred categories focus on serving the needs of students contrasts with the findings of Gross and Grambsch [32] when they ranked the goal perceptions of approximately 15,000 university administrators and faculty members in 1964. Only one of the seven top-ranked goals of universities was concerned in any way with students, and "that one—the output goal of training students for research and scholarship—is closely associated with the scholarly interest of professors and with the emphasis given to pure research." [32, p. 30] Universities, at least in 1964, gave scant attention to the interests of students, in contrast to the number of high-ranking student-oriented goals emphasized by the community junior college presidents. This is a very significant difference.

Among the presidents' five lowest-ranked goal items in both the present and preferred categories are the following two statements: (1) Helping to formulate programs in a number of public policy areas, and (2) Attempting to solve the economic, political, and social needs of the surrounding community. "Attracting a representative number of minority faculty members" and "allocating percent of enrollment for minority groups" also draw little support from presidents. That these goal items represent areas of considerable controversy is demonstrated by the variations in responses. Three of the four mean scores (in terms of present emphasis) were above a standard deviation of 1.0, making it difficult to judge just what normative score to assign to these goal items. "Allocating a percentage of the enrollment for minority or low socioeconomic groups" may very well be perceived as running counter to state statutes or federal regulations. The ambivalent attitudes on this item may very well occur because of the ambiguity of the statement (even though it had been carefully pretested before inclusion in the survey instrument). Those who are strongly committed to a policy of open enrollment might understandably interpret this particular goal statement as ultimately leading to enrollment constraints which would militate against equal access for all students regardless of race, creed, or color. The variability of responses does demonstrate the diversity of views associated with this goal statement.

"Formulating programs in the public interest" and "attempting to solve social or economic problems in the immediate geographic area," while they ranked low among the present and preferred goals of presidents, do not involve the same degree of controversy that minority group enrollments or minority representation on the faculty involve.[3] While there have been pressures from community groups on their local community colleges to respond to such needs, it is apparent that the presidents do not feel that such concerns are to be given top priority.[4] Note the degree of congruence between the present and the preferred ratings. Community representatives perhaps need to generate stronger pressures for social and economic reform programs if they want to bring attention to these issues during the coming decade.

Two goal items stand out as over- or underemphasized. The first, "ensuring faculty participation in institutional decision making," moves from a relatively high rank under the perceived column to a considerably lower-ranked position in the preferred column (twelfth to nineteenth). As we have already observed, presidents seem to feel that faculty groups have been given too much power in this area and that such power might better be shared with other concerned groups, such as trustees or students. The second goal item, upon which presidents feel there ought to be a good deal more emphasis, is the concern with "reeducating and retraining those whose vocational capabilities are obsolete." This item is ranked twelfth among the preferred goals but falls to the twentieth rank in terms of present emphasis. The high variance in perceptions on how much emphasis is currently being given this goal is attributable to the presidents of private junior colleges, who are not at all sure that this is a practice which their institutions ought to be emphasizing. Removing the 20 private junior college presidents from the sample reduces the variance on the perceived goal from 1.10 to .92 (see Appendix D for a comparison of public and private two-year college presidents' views on these statements). When private junior college presidents' views are excluded, this goal statement rises to the upper third among goals supported by public community college presidents.

The high variance on the lowest present and perceived goal, "strengthening the religious faith of students," reflects the different

---

[3] In order to assess the contrasting views of chief executives from public and private institutions on these and other policy issues, see page 58 and Appendix D.

[4] Presidents of public community colleges do give a high ranking to the goal statements "to be responsive to the needs of the local community" and "to serve the higher education needs of youth from the surrounding community" (first and second rank in both the "preferred" and the "present" categories), but both statements tend to reflect the more conventional commitments of their institutions. Adult education also falls among the top third of their priorities. Obviously, these community needs are being responded to, possibly because they represent the more accepted "bread and butter" services that a community college is expected to provide, and possibly because there is a greater expressed need in these areas on the part of the community.

perspective of the few presidents who preside over religiously affiliated junior colleges. Removal of this subgroup of presidents from the total distribution reduces the variance considerably. For those representing public community colleges or independent junior colleges this is clearly a goal which is no longer felt to have much relevance to postsecondary education.

PUBLIC AND PRIVATE JUNIOR COLLEGES: A CONTRAST

By comparing the perceptions of presidents in public and private two-year colleges, we find that the private junior college presidents place greater stress on the intellectual, psychological, and moral development of the student, while public community college presidents are more concerned with career education, adult education, and responding to the needs of the local community. Paralleling these findings, the rank order assigned to the present and preferred output goals revealed that the goals of "helping students respect their own abilities and limitations" and "maintaining an atmosphere of intellectual excitement" fall into the top third of the private junior college presidents' goals, while they occupy positions in the middle ranks for public community college presidents. "Encouraging students to undertake self-directed study," while ranked among the middle third by private junior college presidents, is still ranked significantly higher by them than by their counterparts in the public two-year institutions. This concern with developing the student's objectivity and inculcating a desire to study independently parallels the more traditional commitments of the private four-year colleges and universities.

Private junior college presidents are also much more concerned with "increasing the number and diversity of sources of income," "clearly defining institutional purposes," and "encouraging mutual trust and respect among faculty, students, and administrators." Public community college presidents, on the other hand, tend to value egalitarian goals such as "making financial assistance available to any student who wants to enroll in college," "providing some form of education for any student regardless of his academic ability," and "helping students adapt to new occupational requirements." While this is not meant to imply that private junior colleges are any less student-oriented than their counterparts in the public domain, it does point up the fact that the presidents of these institutions are less likely to be concerned with opening their doors to all applicants, regardless of their qualifications.

These findings, when compared with those of the Gross and Grambsch study, reveal several interesting parallels between private and public universities and private and public two-year colleges:

Private institutions concern themselves with cultivating the student's intellect . . . developing his objectivity about himself and his beliefs. In public universities, on the other hand, no student-expressive goals received particular emphasis. With respect to student-instrumental goals, private universities stress providing students with skills, attitudes, contracts, and experiences which maximize the likelihood of their achieving high status . . . whereas public universities stress preparing students for useful careers. . . . State universities give priority to carrying on applied research, assisting citizens through extension programs and similar services, and providing cultural leadership to the community through programs in the arts, public lectures, exhibits, and so forth. . . . Private universities are more interested in students of high potential whereas public universities concern themselves with educating all high school graduates who meet the legal requirements for admission. Moreover, the public universities emphasize satisfying the needs and solving the problems of the immediate geographical region—a goal closely connected to the direct service goal of providing extension services—and keeping costs as low as possible. . . . [32, pp. 47-48]

They attribute the elitist orientation of the private institutions to the influence that deans and faculty have on decision making, in contrast with state universities and public colleges, where outside groups such as the state legislature and boards of regents exercise a relatively higher degree of decision-making authority.

Selectivity and concern with developing the students' intellectual capacities on the part of private junior colleges may, during this period of rampant egalitarianism, serve to fill an important void which has emerged in higher education. Rather than slavishly patterning themselves after four-year colleges or public community colleges, the private junior colleges might well turn adversity into opportunity. Selectivity, while conventionally associated with screening out the low-ability student (as measured by culturally biased standardized achievement tests), might better be exercised along other lines, such as selecting students whose learning habits make them potentially more responsive to other than the traditional verbal mode of instruction. Disadvantaged students, students with poorly developed communication skills, students who speak two or more languages, all are candidates for learning programs tailored to their particular learning styles. While many public institutions of higher education, both two- and four-year, emphasize community service and comprehensive educational programs, private junior colleges, with their relatively higher degree of autonomy and self-directedness, could strengthen their competitive position vis-à-vis other institutions if they aggressively pursued the special student by demonstrating their superior ability to meet his needs. Such an option or alternative might serve as a deterrent to what the Newman report describes as the tendency to transform "community institutions into amorphous, bland, increasingly large, increasingly state dominate, two-year institutions which serve a number of interests other than that of students." [52, p. 74] A wide range of program offerings by public two-year institutions has not lessened the appeal of proprietary vocational schools which make it their business to offer up-to-date and effective occupational training. For reasons already noted, private junior colleges might well pursue a parallel strategy, zeroing in on special categories of students by offering them learning systems tailored to their needs.

To achieve such an objective will require a new awareness on the part of junior college presidents in contrast to their responses to certain goal statements provided by our study. "Developing programs for the special student, e.g., disadvantaged, bright, foreign" fell well down the list of priorities for both public and private institutions (eighteenth in rank in the preferred category). "Experimenting with new forms of instruction" fared a little better in private junior colleges (eighth in the preferred category) than it did in the public community colleges (fifteenth), indicating a slightly stronger orientation in this direction on the part of private institutions. Most private institutions do not see themselves competing with public or even proprietary vocational schools, as evidenced by the low rank assigned to the goal of "providing a wide range of opportunities for specific occupational preparation" (twenty-first on the preferred scale, as contrasted with twelfth on the public institution presidents' ranking). An attempt to move in the direction of alternative offerings will require an ordering of priorities different from that which presently prevails.

Faculty groups at public and private two-year institutions on the whole evidence greater agreement in their views of what ought to be and what are the goals of their institutions than do presidents. Appendix D presents the detailed breakdown of their responses to the 12 goal statements. Both institutional groups strongly endorse, for example, "helping students to develop a respect for their own abilities and limitations" (although there is some indication that public community college faculty members feel that this goal is honored more in the breach than in the practice). Both groups give stronger backing to the need for "formulating programs in a number of public policy areas such as pollution control and urban renewal" than do presidents; however, both faculty groups see a gap between what ought to be and the current practice. And both groups feel that their institutions are putting too much emphasis on admitting all applicants regardless of their academic abilities.

There are a few interesting differences between faculties at public and private institutions, differences which follow the same pattern of egalitarian-elitist orientation discussed earlier. "Faculty involvement in decision making" is ranked higher in both the preferred and present practice categories by the faculties of private junior colleges (second and fourth respectively) than by those at the public community colleges (sixth and eighth). There is a slight tendency for more faculty in public institutions than in private institutions to give greater weight to "responding to the needs of the local community" and "reeducating and retraining those whose vocational capabilities are obsolete." One exception to these otherwise consistent findings is in the area of "making financial assistance available to any student who wants to enroll in college." Private junior college faculty members rank it sixth among their preferred goals, while public college faculty members rank it ninth. Both groups rank this statement fifth in terms of present emphasis. One explanation for this apparent discrepancy may lie in the observation that private institutions exercise greater control over the types of financial support available to them and are therefore able to put this policy into practice more readily than public institutions.[5] Not all faculty members at the private institutions concur in this judgment, as evidenced by the high variance in opinions reported for the preferred and present response categories. Such a priority may well represent the "goal" of a few private institutions but should not be described as one of the major "purposes" of private junior colleges collectively (see footnote 2, page 47, for a full definition of these two terms).

STUDENT PERCEPTIONS

An additional important segment of the community junior college scene not yet reported in our analysis concerns the perceptions of students. The two-year college student marches to a different drummer.

The rash of protests by four-year college students in the past few years has tended to overshadow the relative calm experienced on

[5] Reference to the chapter on student characteristics will reveal that proportionally higher numbers of students attending private junior colleges come from low-income families.

many community junior college campuses. While a number of observers have attributed this to the higher level of maturity of the two-year college student, his strong commitment to preparation for a career, and his off-campus residency, part of the credit can also be attributed to the interest shown by faculty in students. Not only is this orientation manifested in the goal priorities already reported for faculty members and presidents, but to a significant extent it is confirmed by the views and opinions of the students.

Table 3.4 establishes the congruency among the top-rated preferred goals responded to by each of our three constituent groups. "Helping students respect their own abilities and limitations," "serving the higher education needs of youth from the local communities," and "helping students adapt to new occupational requirements" are goals which are ranked among the top concerns of full-time students enrolled at the time of the survey. However, two hitherto neglected goals, "making financial assistance available to any student who wants to enroll in college" and "providing some form of education for any student regardless of his academic ability," are given a much higher ranking by students than by either faculty or presidents. These findings tend to support the observation made earlier that the younger generation is more egalitarian in its outlook than "establishment" representatives and supports those policies and practices which facilitate that end.

Two goals which received particular attention—one because of its overemphasis by the institutions involved in the survey and the other because of its underemphasis—reflect the growing concern on the part of students with the internal power structure and the community orientation of their institutions. Students rank as sixth on their list of preferred goals the "formulation of public policy programs in such areas as pollution control, urban renewal, and health care." However, when ranked in terms of the current emphasis that community colleges are giving to this area of concern, it falls almost at the bottom of their list. "Ensuring faculty participation in decision making" suffers a reverse priority. Students ranked it tenth on their list of preferred goals and sixth in terms of current emphasis by their institutions. The implications of this latter situation have already been discussed. The former concern suggests that the formulation of public policy programs needs to be given more attention by both faculty and presidents. It is worth noting that the degree of emphasis, as measured by the similarity of the mean scores on a five-point scale, is quite comparable from one group to the other; only the rank order of this goal statement differs significantly.

The low rank accorded the two goal statements concerned with minorities was, at first blush, surprising. Since the majority of students are white, however, these concerns may not occupy their attention or interest to the extent that they would minority groups. Unfortunately, our limited budget did not permit extensive cross-tabulations with controls on minority group status. Consequently, such a conjecture must await additional analysis beyond that intended (or budgeted for) by the study.

A second interpretation may reside in the ambiguity of the wording of these two goal statements, particularly the one dealing with the setting of quotas to enhance the potential enrollment of minority groups. As has been pointed out, if such a policy were carried to its logical conclusion, it would clearly contradict the larger commitment of community colleges to the policy of equal access of any student, regardless of his academic ability or background, to a postsecondary education. The recruitment of faculty members who are identified with minority groups to be served in the community might be interpreted by some students as creating a climate in which faculty selection standards would be compromised in order to accommodate these demands. In any event, the response of students to these two goal statements puts them squarely on record as endorsing the same low-priority status for these items as do the presidents and faculty groups.

SUMMARY

There is a high degree of consensus among community junior college administrators, faculty, and students on the major goals to be served by their colleges. Differences do occur, however. Presidents emphasize responding to community needs; faculty place greater stress upon the student's personal development; and students press for more egalitarian goals, like the concept of the "open door" and expanded financial aid.

Community junior college presidents place significantly greater weight on output goals (i.e., changes in student performance) than do university administrators. Only one of seven top-ranked goals of university administrators focused on serving the needs of students, according to an earlier survey, while five of the top third (5 out of 9) of the community junior college presidents' goals are student-oriented. Recruiting minority faculty members and allocating a percentage of the student enrollment for minority groups or those from low socioeconomic backgrounds fails to draw much support and appears to be among the more controversial goal statements presented to the respondents. Formulating programs in the public interest and attempting to solve social or economic problems in the immediate geographic area, while they do not spark the same degree of controversy as the previously mentioned items, also fail to attract presidential backing. Community leaders hoping to involve their local community junior college need to argue for such concerns more effectively.

The presidents of private junior colleges place greater stress on the intellectual, psychological, and moral development of the student, while public community college presidents are more concerned with occupational, adult, and college-parallel programs for residents of the local community. Private junior college presidents, like their four-year counterparts, tend to be more elitist in their views, while community college presidents, on the other hand, value egalitarian goals. The private junior colleges' concern with selectivity might very well be turned to their advantage if such institutions focused their attention on students with special needs, e.g., students with poorly developed communication skills, students who speak English as a second language, disadvantaged students, etc. While many public institutions stress comprehensiveness, private junior colleges, with their higher degree of autonomy and self-directedness, could strengthen their competitive position if they aggressively recruited students with special needs by demonstrating their ability to tailor learning opportunities to such needs.

Faculty at both public and private colleges strongly endorse helping students to develop a high degree of self-awareness and respect for their own abilities. Both groups give stronger backing to the need for aiding the community in problems of pollution control and urban renewal than do presidents, but, unlike the presidents, faculty members feel that their institutions are putting too much emphasis on admitting all applicants regardless of their academic abilities. There is a tendency for private junior college faculties to follow the same pattern of elitist orientation as their chief executive officers. Public community college faculties put greater stress on responding to the needs of the local communities and upon vocational training and retraining.

Full-time students endorse many of the top-ranked goals of presidents and faculty but give their primary support to making financial assistance available to any student who wants to enroll. Providing some form of education for any student regardless of his academic ability was also ranked higher, thus supporting the contention that students are more egalitarian in their views than the "establishment."

The next chapter will propose a framework which individual institutions can use to conduct their own discrepancy analysis, building upon the type of data presented here. Institutional profiles comparing student, faculty, and presidents' views will be suggested as a starting point for aligning current practices with preferred goals in a systematic manner.

Chapter 4. Strategies for Change

During the decade of the 1970s, community colleges will be faced with a set of demands different from those they experienced during the past two decades. The concern with building new facilities and providing ample classroom space is being replaced by concern for greater equality of educational opportunities and curricula tailored to the needs of students with varying aptitudes and ability levels. College administrators and staff are responding to these challenges by adopting instructional programs and procedures that are designed to effectively serve *student* needs, not simply those of the instructor. While it may be fashionable to deride educators for their resistance to change, it may be more accurate to lay the blame at the feet of those responsible for the development of alternative programs—would-be innovators who fail to design a "total package" that can be readily adopted. It is the purpose of this chapter to set forth the criteria by which new programs and materials can be judged as improvements on current practices are sought out and evaluated.

Past efforts at improving community junior colleges have tended to deal with fragments of the total system. Such efforts often failed to become fully accepted because they brought pressure to bear on other traditional ways of doing things, with the result that those with vested interest in the "tried and true" methods resisted the proposed change for fear their jobs would be put in jeopardy. Small-scale changes had minimum impact because they dealt with only a part of the total learning process. What was needed was a total systems approach where piecemeal improvements could be linked together by means of a well-thought-out strategy for change.

Fortunately, a systems-analytic approach does provide a way of relating "output" to "process." It is not a new or magic formula, nor does it guarantee success. The basic concept—frequently described as a rational problem-solving approach—has proven to be a powerful tool in the hands of operations researchers and systems analysts. Are these techniques applicable to the problems of community junior colleges? What insights do they offer which will aid decision makers in their search for improvements?

IS A SYSTEMS APPROACH TO EDUCATIONAL REFORM POSSIBLE?

To the experienced college staff member, it is obvious that there are some similarities and some significant differences between educational systems and other types of organizations. A large community college must acquire and allocate resources, schedule classes and students, hire and assign staff, and plan ahead—functions which most large-scale organizations must cope with. However, when it comes to introducing a new ethnic studies program into the curriculum, a host of problems not likely to be found in other institutional settings are encountered. Faculty become concerned that the required courses in American History, for example, will lose their appeal and may even be eliminated from the prescribed curriculum for lack of enrollees. Students become frustrated because the new courses are offered at inconvenient times. For example, black students at one southeastern campus were convinced that an ethnic studies course was being offered in the afternoon on purpose so that those who had to work in the afternoon would not be able to attend. Counselors become frustrated because those who do enroll may fail to measure up to standard achievement norms. Regional accrediting groups are not able to decide whether the new curriculum meets their criteria of excellence. Boards of trustees, in their concern over increasing demands on the educational dollar, become concerned about the cost of setting up a new curriculum. They worry about the overall quality of the educational program and whether an ethnic studies course indicates a trend toward the lowering of academic standards. These are a few of the issues that will be raised when a new course offering is contemplated.

What are some of the differences between educational organizations generally and those organizations where systems-analytic techniques have proved to be helpful? Cogan [19] identifies five essential differences: (1) The types of large-scale, expensive development programs in which systems analysis has played an important role are usually administered by a centralized management structure such as is found in the military or in private industry (America's school system is largely decentralized and pluralistic); (2) dollar resources available to educators are frequently inadequate to support a large-scale innovative effort; (3) most innovations in education have not been made fully operational—the packaging is inadequate; (4) systems analysts and related specialists have only recently arrived on the educational scene, and they are in short supply; (5) education is fundamentally a human enterprise. Systematic problem-solving techniques used in the design of hardware need to be drastically modified when employed in the prediction of human behavior. For these reasons, extreme caution must be used in any attempt to transfer systems-analytic methods from one realm to another.

Let us look at the military training command as an example. It trains its personnel to a specific level of competence in a particular job skill. Most of the trainees are reasonably well motivated high school graduates. They are assured that they will be permitted to pursue the particular occupation for which they are being trained provided they are reasonably diligent in their efforts. The skills required to operate a new weapons system are determined well in advance so that training materials, workbooks, and instructional procedures can be carefully prepared. The performance of graduates can be monitored and the results fed back to the training command if improvements are required. The hierarchical nature of the decision-making command structure makes it likely that a well-designed training program will be adopted throughout the total command. Heavy start-up costs can be amortized across large numbers of men and materials.

This brief comparison is meant to point up a few of the differences between the centrally controlled and efficient military training command and our largely decentralized and locally managed educational system. To realize those differences may be to realize the problems involved in applying a systems-analytic approach to educational improvements. Modifying an ongoing educational system is difficult because of the number of uncontrolled variables involved. Until recently, few educators have been capable of even verifying which educational practices are the most valid. The recent formulation of a theory of planned change in education does offer at least the possibility of plotting needed reforms in a systematic way. This, together with the availability of improved methods of assessing individual student progress, makes it more likely today that innovative programs will be readily institutionalized, although in the past they generally have not been.

GOALS AND THEIR ASSESSMENT

All organizations—profit-making, nonprofit, high schools, and colleges—have something in common—they all have goals. All too often these goals are not well understood by the members of the organization. International Business Machines, for example, ought to be and is certainly successful in achieving its goals. An employee opinion survey conducted in one of IBM's plants, however, demonstrated that a large number of its employees had no idea what the product of the plant production effort was and how their particular responsibility linked with that product. Other organizations state one set of goals but their practices belie that commitment.

Most educational institutions, be they elementary, secondary, or postsecondary institutions, find it difficult to evaluate their own performance because of their failure to state goals and related objectives in ways that lend themselves to assessment. Goal achievement often depends upon the care with which subsystem objectives are specified. Subsystem or intermediate objectives can be used by faculty members to guide students as they progress through a given subject matter toward "terminal" performance objectives. The goals toward which performance objectives are pointed represent the longer-range mission of an instructional program and provide an integrative theme for the learning program as a whole.

Three comments need to be made regarding the present effort to focus attention upon performance assessment as the major criterion for determining the effectiveness of a school. First, many of the earlier efforts to determine a school's productivity consisted of counting the number of books in the library and the number of teachers with master's degrees. Effectiveness was measured in terms of how well a program was being implemented, and this restricted the consideration of alternative teaching strategies to reshuffling time-worn practices of the past. Restating objectives in terms of "output," or changes in the learner's performance, offers the advantage of relating inputs and instructional processes to results, with close attention to the interaction between these three classes of variables.

Second, broader educational goals, stated in the terms of the behavior which students should evidence upon completion of a program of study, need to be broken down into more specific short-term, or interim, "output" objectives which collectively lead to improved student performance. To express these "terminal" objectives in terms of a detailed set of interim objectives is an arduous task, demanding considerable time investment on the part of the faculty if such objectives are to be built from the ground up.[1]

Third and last, for certain types of learning experiences the learning process itself defines the objective being served. In a number of instances, general goals are all that can be stated, and sub-objectives can only be clarified through experience with individual learners. Self-confidence, a desire to continue one's learning beyond the formal years of schooling, adoption of a set of values compatible with those in a democratic society, all represent outcomes which are difficult to break down into component parts. Yet such goals are obviously an important part of a student's educational development.

Examined from the perspectives of the types of behavior which a student should evidence upon completion of a program of study, many of today's curriculum and instructional procedures should be tagged as inadequate. By converting the broad educational goals of community junior colleges into more specific "output" and "process" objectives, college administrators and faculty should be able to identify a minimum set of skills, knowledge, and attitudes to be achieved by a majority of the students enrolled in a particular course. How is this conversion process to take place? By what alchemy can we move from where we are today to where we would like to be? First the model, then the strategy.

SIX STEPS TOWARD A SYSTEMATIC CHANGE STRATEGY

A new branch of social science has emerged during the past two decades which deals with the transfer and utilization of knowledge. This discipline grew out of the interest of the rural sociologist in the cooperative extension program whereby agricultural extension agents served as intermediaries between the agricultural experimental stations and the farmer. The extension agent was trained to inform

---

[1] The Center for the Study of Evaluation at UCLA has established an Instructional Objectives Exchange under the direction of Dr. W. James Popham to deposit, develop, and disseminate measurable objectives and items for use by educators. They hope to be able to provide teachers with well-conceived output objectives to be employed in the redesign of curriculum materials.

and persuade his client, the farmer, that adopting a new seed or farming procedure would be in the farmer's best interest. Further elaboration of this relatively simple model led to the development of "linkage" strategies for bringing complex knowledge and scientific developments from resource groups to user groups.

Those associated with this area of study have generally advocated one of three models for the implementation of intervention strategy. Each of these three models can be described briefly as follows:

1 Research, Development and Diffusion Model. Advocates of this approach emphasize the careful development, evaluation, and packaging of information for use by practitioners. They assume that a well-designed procedure or application will, in effect, sell itself to potential users. Awareness of the barriers, human fears, and needs of the user group is frequently absent. A better mousetrap, they argue, will capture its own audience.

2 Social Interaction Model. Advocates of this position draw heavily upon the research of Kurt Lewin, Herbert Thelan, Dorwin Cartwright, Ronald Lippitt, and others interested in group dynamics. By identifying opinion leaders and noting their influence on others within a social group, advocates of this position argue, the flow of new information and its impact can be charted and predicted. There is little evidence of their concern, however, with how carefully and accurately the information communicated was initially developed. They are principally concerned with user needs and not with the research and development stages associated with the initial input of information.

3 Problem-solving Model. This more rationalistic approach to facilitating the dissemination and utilization of information grew out of attempts to apply systems-analytic procedures to social problems. It also starts with the assumption that user needs are paramount but then prescribes a step-by-step problem-solving procedure which the practitioner is expected to follow while he attempts to diagnose the problem, search for alternatives, evaluate alternatives, and ultimately implement the most suitable strategy for change. As such, this model puts excessive pressure on the user to carry through the problem-solving steps designated. It does not provide for the exploitation of existing information or outside resource groups. Nor is there adequate attention given to the "human relations" problems which arise when one attempts to proceed in an impersonal, systematic manner.

Ronald Havelock [35] undertook to review and synthesize more than 4,000 studies dealing with the dissemination and utilization process as they might bear upon the problem of facilitating educational change. The more important variables outlined in the above brief summary of the more popular change models were then synthesized into what Havelock has termed the "linkage model." It, too, starts by focusing on the user as a problem solver. The user senses an initial "felt need" which motivates him to diagnose and set forth the elements of the problem that he is experiencing. Through a systematic search process, various alternative solutions are identified and evaluated before a particular solution is selected for trial. During the search stage, the problem solver links up with outside resource groups in the expectation that new and more relevant alternatives will be discovered, offering him the opportunity to test these new approaches. In the process of linking with outside resource groups, the problem solver must enter into a reciprocal relationship if the link is to be optimally productive; in other words, the resource group as well as the user must be aware of the situation in which the problem solver operates if they are to react productively. The resource group, in effect, simulates the need-reduction cycle of the user. Not only must they be able to simulate the user's needs, but they must also be able to simulate the search activity which the user is going through. Potential solutions need to be tested out in much the same way that the user himself would test them. Havelock argues that only in this way can a resource person understand and link effectively with the user.

Linkage is not simply a two-person interaction process, however; the resource person, in turn, must have access to more remote and more expert resources than himself. In his efforts to aid the user, the resource person finds it necessary to draw upon other specialists. He must develop a means of communicating his need for knowledge to other resource persons, and these in turn must have the capacity, at least to a limited degree, to recapitulate the problem-solving cycle already outlined. Only in this fashion can the more remote members of the communication chain develop their own reciprocal relationship with each link in the chain.

There is a growing consensus among students of planned change that a problem-solving and a human relations approach to decision making must be merged before a truly functional change model can evolve. Such a concept was recently proposed by William D. Hitt [38] at the 1972 AACJC convention in Dallas, Texas. It was Hitt's thesis that a rationally planned problem-solving process will not succeed without careful consideration of the personal feelings, motives, and values of those involved. He argues that "underlying the humanistic management philosophy is the basic proposition that the human dimension of management and the scientific dimension can be effectively united through participative management." [38, p. 11]

It is important to involve those people who have a vital interest in a given program, such as students, faculty, administrators, or even the community at large. To the extent that such groups are actively a part of the planning process, a systematic strategy for change is more likely to be successful. The greater the extent of involvement of individuals in the development of output objectives, for example, the more likely will be their commitment to the achievement of those objectives. The utility of the Havelock linkage model is that it not only takes into account the importance of the interpersonal linkage between user groups and resource groups, but also moves beyond the static description of knowledge transfer inherent in the RD&D model. It also incorporates the important elements of a systematic problem-solving approach with the planned intervention strategies implicit in the social interaction model.

Having adopted the linkage model as a guide, what are the basic steps through which a problem solver[2] should proceed as he attempts to go about implementing needed reforms within his institution? What follows is an overview of a series of suggested steps. Each problem solver will want to test out such a procedure in the real world of the college. Six steps make up this problem-solving strategy:[3]

1 Diagnosing the problem
2 Formulating objectives and criteria of effectiveness
3 Identifying constraints and needed resources
4 Selecting potential solutions
5 Evaluating these alternative solutions
6 Implementing the selected alternatives within the college system

Each step will be discussed briefly and, where relevant, examples will be introduced to illustrate each step under consideration.

Step One: Diagnosing the Problem

A successful planned change strategy begins with the recognition that a problem exists. While this may seem self-evident, many efforts at reform fail because those responsible for carrying out the problem-

---

[2] The problem solver referred to could be the chief executive officer, a dean, or anyone in a policy-making position. A number of larger institutions now have "change agents" who have been directed to help spur others in the organization toward the adoption of needed reforms. A problem solver could be one of these functionaries.

[3] The following discussion draws heavily upon a chapter entitled "Organizing For Change" in David S. Bushnell and Donald Rappaport, *Planned Change in Education* (New York: Harcourt Brace Jovanovich, 1971).

solving effort are unable to cut through to the central issues and needs involved. In Chapter 2, for example, we discovered a sizable discrepancy between student and faculty perceptions of the utility of the pupil personnel services program. Some guidance counselors might be disposed to pass this off as simply evidence of the students' inability to grasp the significance of the complexity of the decision-making process associated with arriving at a career commitment. Yet several studies have shown that the community college student derives little benefit from the occupational counseling available to him. [57] Furthermore, guidance counselors are often unaware of the level of decision making a student has arrived at as he attempts to cope with a variety of options or lack of options. The failure of faculty members, and to some extent guidance counselors themselves, to recognize the importance of outside influences in career decision making leads them to place considerable value on the availability of guidance services to students. But this same mistake is not made by students, thus the discrepancy. The roles of parents, teachers, business and industry representatives, labor unions, and even TV and the print media need to be given greater weight in the career guidance equation. Providing students with access to the typical pupil personnel program represents only one way of getting at a rather complex decision-making process. A successful problem-solving strategy must be able to sort out the many variables which operate in this situation if it is to successfully explain the discrepancies in perceptions cited in the earlier chapter.

Closely tied to the problem of diagnosis is the need to pinpoint just who the appropriate persons to be involved in the diagnostic process are. Who are the opinion molders and leaders? What are their perceptions and needs? Simply accepting their off-the-top-of-the-head interpretation of a problem, however, would be akin to a medical practitioner accepting uncritically the patient's self-diagnosis of an illness. The problem solver not only must tap the important persons for their perceptions of the problem, but must also interpret that information in light of current theory. Some of the more obvious and pressing problems reflecting what is and what ought to be happening at community colleges can be summarized as follows:

1 Many academically trained faculty members are disposed to favor the college transfer student. Reared in the tradition of the liberal arts, such faculty members often have negative attitudes toward occupational courses. Since many of these same people are tapped to fill administrative positions, their institutions tend to relegate occupational training programs to a position of lesser prestige. Too frequently, this attitude is communicated to the students.

2 Perhaps the most glaring gap between goal and practice is in the area of general education. Little emphasis is placed upon interdisciplinary studies in areas where a broad base of learning skills needs to be developed to tackle emergent social problems, such as pollution control, solid waste management, and transportation. While there is some evidence (reported later) that college departments are beginning to be structured along interdisciplinary lines, much remains to be done, particularly in such areas as the humanities and social sciences.

3 The community service area is often an ancillary part of the community college. There is meager financial support for such efforts, and what resources are available are sometimes cut back when the institution is faced with a budget crunch. Some programs have little relevance to community needs or constituent groups. In fact, meeting community needs often means responding to the special interest of middle-class business and professional groups without recognition of the concerns of other segments of the community.

4 Heterogeneous student populations are difficult to handle in the typical classroom situation. Instructional procedures and curricula are often geared to one group of students, e.g., the college transfer student. Little provision is made for differentiating between the verbally and non-verbally-oriented student nor between the self-starters and the other-directed students. High attrition rates still persist, particularly among those from educationally disadvantaged backgrounds.

This brief recounting of some of the problems currently being confronted by community junior college administrators is meant to demonstrate that there is a continuing need for change. Those who occupy key decision-making roles are groping for better ways to operate. The solution will not be found by simply changing the organizational structure or by appointing new investigating committees. Basic changes require a careful diagnosis and identification of the underlying causes within a total system framework.

Step Two: Formulating Objectives

Having identified and teased out the important variables involved in a particular problem area and having inventoried the perceptions of key persons involved, a search for alternative solutions can begin. Before undertaking such a search, however, the problem solver must first decide what improvements he is trying to achieve and what his goals and objectives are. As defined earlier, an objective may be the end of an action or an intermediate step directed toward a more distant goal. Well-stated curriculum objectives, for example, should describe in operational or behavioral terms the types of behavior desired, state the criteria of acceptable performance, be consistent with longer-term goals, and specify the conditions under which the desired behavior needs to be performed. This set of criteria helps to illustrate the essential differences between goals or general objectives and more specific objectives which are capable of quantification.

As we observed in the previous chapter, students, faculty, and administrators show a growing degree of consensus on the goals to be served by a comprehensive community junior college program. These can be briefly summarized as follows:

1 The university parallel program provides a full range of academic offerings paralleling the lower division undergraduate programs of four-year colleges. Such courses should be fully transferable on completion of an Associate of Arts degree and should be equal in every way to college courses at other institutions.

2 The general education program gives enrolled students the opportunity to obtain a broad general education, equivalent to the traditional concept of a liberal education. A graduate should possess the learning skills and study habits which will aid him during his adult years. Basic and intermediate-level courses in the arts, humanities, and sciences should be studied, with the intent of developing a full range of intellectual skills.

3 Occupational or career education programs should be provided, offering students the opportunity to develop entry-level job skills which match the employment needs of the larger community. Cooperative education programs, work/study programs, and placement services should acquaint students with the environmental conditions and background requirements if a qualified graduate is to enter and advance in his chosen career field. Part-time and continuing education students should have access to upgrading and retraining opportunities designed to enhance their success as they attempt to climb a career ladder.

4 The open-door philosophy of the community college should ensure that students of widely varying interests, motivations, and ability levels will be served. Most public community colleges limit entrance qualifications to a high school diploma or equivalent, and for the most part require little or no tuition. Developmental or compensatory education programs should be provided for those who need remedial assistance.

5 The lifelong learning and community service function of a community college should clearly be geared to the special requirements and needs of the community. Most community colleges recognize this requirement by providing college-level courses during evening hours, cooperative programs with industry for career upgrading, special programs for low-income groups, and noncredit courses for those wishing to pursue avocational or cultural interests.

6 Cutting across all the previously mentioned goals should be a continuous

program of career counseling. Viewed as an essential part of the comprehensive college program, the counseling and guidance function should serve the student from preregistration through graduation or beyond.

This recital of the more conventional goals of community junior colleges disguises what is perhaps the more difficult task of breaking these goal statements down into specific, measureable objectives. A brief summary of the common management problems experienced in attempting to state objectives is appropriate here. These have been outlined in a more complete form elsewhere. [12]

First, an objective should be stated in quantifiable or, if relevant, behavioral terms. It should be stated precisely and contain only one element of the total problem. It should describe or imply the completion of certain actions which are assessible.

Second, an objective should describe what is to be done, how it is to be done, and with what degree of acceptability. For example, a well-stated curriculum objective might be to require that a student complete a 100-item multiple-choice test on the principles of "management by objectives." The lower limit of acceptable performance might be 85 correct items completed within a time span of 90 minutes.

Third, a well-stated objective is internally consistent, that is, it is consistent with other goals and objectives of the organization.

Fourth, objectives should be consistent with what is intended. The layman can seldom decide whether or not a given procedure or practice is consistent with what the educational institution is trying to accomplish. The college administrator or the faculty members should be responsible for deciding whether a given objective will help students achieve their particular goals. Determining the consistency between the objective and what is actually intended requires expert judgment or empirical validation.

Fifth, objectives should be comprehensive. Sometimes efforts are directed at the achievement of two or three objectives while others are ignored. It is important that the sum total of objectives be sufficiently comprehensive to cover all the significant aspects of the problem. One of the dangers in the use of programmed instruction, for example, is that, as students are required to proceed in a stepwise fashion—one step at a time—toward the achievement of some specific learning objective, they may, in the process, be taught to avoid the inductive leaps which are so often a part of that important "ah hah" experience in learning. The consequences of prescribing a programmed instruction learning sequence should be anticipated in advance, if possible.

Sixth, objectives should provide for individual differences. Some faculty members believe that if they develop a specific set of objectives, all students must work toward the same level of accomplishment in the same manner. This does not always have to be the case, however. Ideally, objectives should be tailored to the individual needs, interests, abilities, and background of the student.

Each student's performance should be evaluated with respect to how well he is doing in the light of that objective formulated specifically for him. At the time he completes his program of study, each student should be assured that he does qualify for a job or that he can go on to college if he chooses and that he will be able to compete successfully when there. To ensure his continuing adaptability, he needs to be reasonably proficient in the basic learning skills.

Seventh, objectives must take into consideration the real world and its constraints. State laws, shortages of tax funds, or unavailable faculty members may block the achievement of a given objective if they are not anticipated and taken into account.

Eighth, and last, objectives should be obtainable but ambitious enough to be challenging. In football, a good pass is one which is thrown just far enough in front of the receiver that he has to stretch a little and is challenged to reach it. Obviously, if the receiver has to stand and wait for the pass or cannot get to it, it is not likely to be completed. Suffice it to say that the participants in a problem-solving effort must be convinced that the objectives toward which they are moving are worth the effort. Collaborative effort will help to ensure the full commitment of all who are involved, which will in turn help to ensure a successful outcome.

Step Three: Identifying Constraints and Needed Resources

Before proceeding to the search for potential solutions and the outlining of a strategy for change, the problem solver must make himself fully aware of the history and traditions which surround a given problem. Constraints and needed resources must be identified. They tend to operate as two sides of the same coin. Lack of a required resource may become a constraint. Faculty attitudes may be positive or negative. State regulations may facilitate or hinder the adoption of new procedures. Thus, either can be classified under one or more of the following categories:

1 Financial considerations (assets and liabilities)
2 Laws and regulations (federal, state, and local)
3 Human considerations (aptitudes, experience, attitudes, limitations)

4 Timing considerations (priorities, previous commitments, deadlines)
5 Demographic considerations (environmental, cultural, natural resources, transportation)
6 Facilities (school plant, classroom equipment, instructional aids, communication facilities)

Specifying the constraints or the setting in which the problem is lodged is often a time-consuming and certainly an important phase of the problem-solving process. Much of Project Focus was concerned with identifying existing conditions and problems. A carefully developed inventory of constraints and needed resources not only serves as a means of pointing up the need for alternative solutions to a problem, but also helps in the elimination of potential alternatives without further analysis.

Needed resources may take the form of information needs, people with special talents, new instructional procedures, or money. Identifying and marshaling the required resources in advance of when they are needed will do much to ensure the successful implementation of a proposed reform.

Step Four: Selecting Potential Solutions

Having successfully analyzed the underlying concerns, identified who would be involved in the problem-solving process, stated the specific objectives, and pinpointed possible barriers and constraints as well as needed resources, the problem solver is now ready to locate and evaluate alternative solutions. Two important procedures need to be implemented in carrying out this step: (1) Reviewing appropriate information sources, and (2) choosing from among an array of promising alternatives the best solution for further analysis. A systematic review of the monthly publication *Research in Education* or utilization of the ERIC clearinghouses, which cover a wide range of topics, makes the task far easier than it would have been a decade ago. Visiting innovative institutions, reviewing evaluative reports, and scanning journals and monographs represent other typical search procedures.

One caveat to be observed: Be wary of the blandishments of outside experts. Such resource people should be able to grapple with and understand a problem in its natural context. Frequently a university-based consultant fails to appreciate the traditions and commitments under which community college administrators are required to operate. He is often more concerned with generalizing from specific situations. On the other hand, practitioners are often disposed to reject solutions proposed by "ivory tower" consultants because their recommendations are phrased in ways that are not easily understood and put to work. Even non-university-based researchers, in their concern with advancing knowledge in their chosen field, tend to delay practical decisions in the interest of accuracy and truth. The problem solver will, in all probability, want to operate within a specific framework and time frame. Effective linkage between a user group and outside resource people requires mutual understanding, equal commitment, and frequent interaction.

Step Five: Evaluating Alternatives

Selecting one or more alternatives from among an array of possible lines of action necessarily requires the establishment of criteria for evaluative purposes. Hopefully, such criteria were agreed upon at the time the attempt at problem solving got under way. However, it is still not too late to establish them. Feasibility, workability, and effectiveness are three of the more common criteria to be employed. Feasibility concerns the likelihood that a given alternative can, in fact, be achieved, keeping in mind the constraints and needed resources available to the group. Workability reflects the extent to which the potential solution really works. How reliable is the proposed procedure? Have the detailed steps to be followed been worked out? What costs are likely to be incurred and can these be met? Incidentally, on this last question, there is a tendency for those who hold the purse strings to impose this selection criterion as a constant while letting alternative strategies vary. It may be just as important to let cost vary until the other assessments have been made. Effectiveness is often the most difficult criterion to employ because of the time lag between a particular demonstration and the expected results. For this reason, judging the effectiveness of one strategy as opposed to another may have to be carried out on a subjective basis. If at all possible, however, objective measures should be employed. Successfully predicting the outcome often requires trained specialists.

A final decision will most likely be based upon a ranking of alternatives by assigning weights to each of these three criteria and then selecting the option that stands out as the most desirable.

Step Six: Implementing the Selected Alternative

Having settled upon a potential solution, the problem solver is now ready to turn over the recommended procedure or strategy to those responsible for implementing the recommendation. Effective follow-up action requires, among other things, early involvement of those who will be assigned the responsibility for implementing the new procedure or practice. This, in turn, requires clear and precise objectives, systematic steps to be followed, and the specification of evaluative criteria; in other words, the same steps through which any systematic problem resolution must proceed. This iterative cycle will continue until the new program is well established.

To ensure continued acceptance of an innovative program, a supportive climate for the project must be maintained. Those responsible must have a sense of confidence and competence, openness to new information, and a willingness to take risks. Anticipated rewards are also an essential ingredient. Recognition as an innovator may be sufficient reward for some. Others will want to see the new program benefiting students. Often the faculty derive little satisfaction from their attempts to help students improve their performance because of the time lag involved before behavioral changes can be ascertained. Frequent measures of interim progress toward a longer-term goal may serve as needed feedback benefiting both students and faculty.

What has been described by these six steps offers a more systematic plan for implementing needed changes within ongoing college programs. Any administrator who considers adopting this planned approach to problem solving may wonder if this is something he does in addition to holding his staff accountable for carrying out their assigned duties. Rather than substituting this procedure for already established mechanisms or procedures for implementing needed reforms, a problem-solving strategy is suggested as a complementary undertaking. It represents a better way of merging rational planning with an active concern for people, and that, of course, is what educational administration is all about.

SUMMARY

A systematic problem-solving approach to educational change has been described as a rational way of relating "input" to "output." To do so requires goals and objectives, a method for evaluating how well those goals are being served, commitment to serving the goals, agreement on how they are to be served, and a mechanism for negotiating new goals and procedures as changing conditions warrant. A system for relating goals to the learning process—by means of a systems-analytic process within a participative management frame-work—provides a more rigorous way of asking and answering questions about how well the college system is functioning. Such a management system can be adopted by implementing six problem-solving, rationally sequenced steps leading to a more effective school program.

The emergence of a more systematic approach to college administration offers the hope of facilitating the realignment of educational priorities for the decade—priorities which commit educators to meeting the needs of all students, not just those who have already learned how to learn. It has been the intent of this chapter to argue for combining the concept of systematic problem solving with the modern management strategies of participative management. Such a synthesis makes it possible to continue our commitment to humanistic goals while improving the productivity of our colleges.

Chapter 5.
Barriers to
Change

The junior college movement emerged at the turn of the century principally as an alternative to the lower-division education programs of colleges and universities. Philosophically, it had its origin in the egalitarian concern for extending educational opportunities to a broader segment of the college-age population on the one hand and strengthening preparatory work for university-level studies on the other. During the period 1900-1925, many junior colleges operated as part of the public school system, with the faculty recruited or reassigned from high schools. Their curriculum and pedagogy was patterned after university lower-division education programs. Following World War I they began to establish their own identity, one that accepted the responsibility for providing both transfer and occupational education. Federal legislation, just prior to World War II, enabled these institutions to launch a uniquely comprehensive education program. During the war, many local junior colleges were given the responsibility for retraining and upgrading defense workers.

Following the Second World War, the GI Bill brought increased pressure on higher educational institutions to expand their enrollments to include returning veterans. Two-year colleges, benefiting from this renewed interest, began to multiply rapidly. California, Florida, North Carolina, and other states adopted statewide plans to ensure a systematic, planned program of expansion. Noncredit adult education programs also emerged as a part of some local two-year colleges' service to their communities. With this addition to the stable of offerings, the prototype comprehensive two-year college was on its way.

As a locally based, community-supported institution, the community junior college was expected to forge a link between high school and four-year institutions. This purpose has been served very well. There are many who now recognize, however, that while this emphasis accommodated the traditional student admirably, the nontraditional student experienced little but frustration as he attempted to gain credit for past experience or to enroll in courses which did not depend upon the traditional group instructional mode. Adult educational programs, for example, often operate in auxiliary or insular fashion. The adult education faculty more often than not are nontenured and paid on an hourly rate, so that when competition for scarce resources forces a choice between the tenured and nontenured faculty, the latter are often the first to be cut back.

The ability of the community junior college to accommodate a diverse set of student needs and a wide range of age groups has not yet been well demonstrated on a nationwide basis. Curriculum content and instructional procedures are clearly oriented to the more able and above-average students. While there is a growing interest in experimental compensatory education programs, [59] few have been carefully evaluated to determine whether they offer a meaningful alternative to current programs. Little provision is being made for differentiating between the verbally skilled and the non-verbally-oriented student, between the career-oriented and the undecided student, or between the part-time student with extensive work experience and the student with little or no experience at all.

Once considered to be in the vanguard of innovative institutions in higher education, community junior colleges are in danger of slipping behind their four-year counterparts. Of twenty-one undergraduate-level external degree programs cited in a recent inventory, only three offered the associate of arts degree and none of these were community or junior colleges. [61]

The "University without Walls" program under the development of the Union of Experimenting Colleges [4] and the recently launched Empire State College program sponsored by the State University of New York [27] are attempting to take students where they are in terms of interests, career plans, and previous experience and help them develop individualized study programs, with or without residence requirements. Moses [51] estimates that within five years, nine times as many adults will be enrolled in nontraditional programs as there are credit students enrolled in the more traditional colleges today. These adults will be engaged in learning activities which are outside the traditional full-time, day-oriented educational system.

It is obvious that community junior colleges have not yet reached the ideal that some have set for them. Four promising lines of development—areas on which, in all probability, the major thrust of the community junior colleges will be directed during the remainder of this decade—have been selected for a closer examination in this chapter. Each area relates closely to the top-ranking goals as perceived by presidents, faculty, and students. The discussion that follows flows primarily out of the many comments and observations which the Project Focus staff gathered during their in-depth interviews with 1,500 or more students, faculty, administrators, board members, community leaders, and state personnel located in thirty community junior colleges in some twenty states.[1] Interview results have been buttressed by the survey data where possible. The reader is encouraged to review what is presented here in the light of his own unique situation and to draw whatever conclusions are relevant. It is hoped that out of this type of more detailed examination, corrective action will begin to be implemented where needed, and community junior colleges will once more occupy a position of leadership.

The four areas of focus—lifelong education, community service, career education, and compensatory education—will be examined from three vantage points: first, what is the current state of the art as revealed by the survey findings and a review of the literature on the topic; second, what are the barriers with which an aspiring change agent must learn to cope if improvements are contemplated; and third, what alternatives ought to be considered if corrective programs are undertaken.

LIFELONG EDUCATION

Current Situation

Among the more important functions of the public community college[2] has been adult and continuing education for those in the

---

[1] For a fuller discussion of these findings, see Gleazer, E. J., Jr., *Project Focus: A Forecast Study of Community Colleges.*

[2] The majority of private junior colleges have not traditionally viewed this activity as one of their major missions.

local community. Five major services have been involved: (1) occupational training, including retraining, occupational upgrading, and preemployment education; (2) avocational and cultural education, providing instruction in leisure-time activities encompassing a wide variety of avocational interests from navigation to the great books; (3) adult basic education, including programs for persons with less than the equivalent of an eighth grade education, usually linked with preemployment training; (4) adult civic education designed to prepare aliens for United States citizenship, sometimes including high school equivalency education; and (5) workshops, seminars, and noncredit courses designed to meet the special needs of the community. Adult education at the community college level does and should play an essential role in helping adults adjust to increased leisure, to changing technological requirements in the work place, and to their civic responsibilities. While such functions may put adult education first in the minds of large numbers of potential enrollees, a look at our survey findings reveals that such a perspective does not square with the priorities of the school administrators.

Presidents of the 90 institutions comprising our sample were asked to assign, under three different budget statuses (stringent, unchanged, and ample), a high, medium, or low priority to a number of college activities. The degree of support for three types of adult programs changes dramatically as the three budget conditions are allowed to vary. Assuming that financial resources were to remain the same over the decade, 51 percent of the presidents responding gave adult evening courses a high priority. Under more constrained financial circumstances, however, only 31 percent did so. Noncredit courses and workshops and seminars received middle-priority ratings should the financial status of the organization stay the same over the decade and slipped dramatically to a low-priority status if financial resources were cut back.

Parallel findings emerged when we examined the ranking of two adult education goal items ("providing education opportunities for adults in the local area" and "reeducate and retrain those whose vocational skills are in danger of becoming obsolete"). The relatively high rank for the retraining goal on the preferred dimension contrasted with its much lower rank in terms of present emphasis (a shift from eighth to sixteenth position). The other adult education goal item suffered a slight reversal in rank, with presidents giving it a rank of 8 on the preferred list and a rank of 5 in terms of their perception of present emphasis.

Faculty and students could also be accused of downgrading the importance of adult education (see Tables 3.3 and 3.4). However, when we consider that the respondents to the survey questionnaire were limited to full-time students and faculty, then this apparent conflict with our earlier claim that adult education occupies an important position in the minds of those in the community becomes more understandable. Such a need was strongly supported by part-time students in many of the interviews which staff members conducted. Since most of these students were older, there was a decided difference between the day and evening students both in the expression of need and in the level of commitment to learning. Adult students were less content with mediocre instructors and more insistent that their individual learning needs be served effectively. They endorsed a free and open exchange between student and instructor and sought out teachers who knew what they were talking about.

A similar conclusion was reached in regard to part-time faculty members. Those interviewed strongly endorsed the need for adult education. Often those who taught in the adult evening or extended day program were recruited directly from the community and therefore were well acquainted with its needs.

It is not sufficient, however, to utilize such "linkage agents" as a systematic means of determining what are appropriate course offerings and support services. Appropriately conceived instructional strategies which reflect the unique requirements of adults must also be incorporated into a program that is committed to adult needs.

Barriers and Constraints

Adult education, unlike other major sectors of public education, has suffered from a proliferation of overlapping institutional support. Extension services of universities, high school-based adult education programs, proprietary schools offering a wide variety of vocational and technical education, and correspondence schools, as well as community colleges, all offer a varied program for the part-time adult student. Short courses offered either in the evening or on a released-time basis, residential programs of a few days or weeks duration, seminars, and coordinated classroom and on-the-job training represent some of the varieties of learning experiences now available. Usually such programs are financed by means of fees or tuition charged directly to the student.

The concept of free continuing education has not yet penetrated the adult education field to any appreciable extent. The fragmented support base and the pay-as-you-go approach tend to limit the amount of federal and state funds flowing into this sector of education. A coordinated lobbying effort by diverse groups of institutional representatives, often with competing interests, has yet to be formed.[3] The result has been limited dollar resources for planning and development purposes.

A second constraint on the more rapid expansion of this area of education has been the peripheral status of such programs within those public institutions where they are lodged. Universities, for example, until recently assigned to continuing education a low status within the departmental hierarchy. Those associated with adult education at the university have traditionally lacked power and influence. While there is some evidence that the status is changing, there has been no dramatic upsurge in the attention given to this relatively nonprestigious sector of higher education.

As we observed in the earlier discussion of the status of the extended day program within community colleges, it is a precarious existence. When faced with the necessity of budget cutbacks, presidents of public community colleges often discover that the only major budgetary item amenable to reduction is the extended day program. Many of the faculty employed in the continuing education program are nontenured, making this one of the more vulnerable budget areas during a budget squeeze. Further evidence of the marginal status of continuing education can be provided by examining state budgets. Only a few states provide separate funds for this purpose. Some money comes from federal appropriations, primarily in the adult basic education area. Duplication and overlapping authorities conspire to dilute the impact of these fragmented programs and detract from their potential appeal to a sizable segment of the adult population.

A third constraint on the development of widespread support for continuing education has been the lack of career ladders or advancement opportunities. Few universities view this area as a top priority. Adult education deans often discover that they have reached the ceiling of their career and that there are very few job slots at higher levels.

A fourth factor, reflecting to some extent the low financial status of this field, is the lack of a well-conceived research and development program aimed at furthering our knowledge of the adult learning

---

[3] There is some hope that this limitation will be overcome by the recent formation of the Adult Education Action Council, purposely organized to represent the interest of all groups concerned with strengthening federal support for adult education.

process. This lack of attention to the particular requirements of adults is highlighted by the tendency of many faculty members to utilize the same type of curriculum and instructional procedures that they employ with younger students. This "warmed over" curriculum and pedagogy frequently creates dissatisfaction on the part of enrolled adults who expected something different.

Future Implications

The necessity for redeploying portions of our labor force from one occupation to another, the continuing effort to improve the socioeconomic status of the disadvantaged segments of our society, and anticipated increases in leisure time have combined to create an unprecedented demand for a wide variety of adult and continuing education opportunities. Many of these are outside the traditional education program. We must look for improved ways of providing nontraditional learning opportunities to meet this increasing demand. Striner [62] has urged the use of unemployment insurance to provide all workers with continuing access to retraining in order to avoid the problems of obsolescence associated with technological change. The search for ways of meeting an anticipated rise in the demand for access to adult study programs has provoked a flurry of innovations, ranging from TV colleges to open universities and external degrees.

   Medsker and Tillery sum up the current status of adult education when they state that

continuing education has a rather shallow meaning if the programs for transfer and occupational students alike do not stimulate interest in lifelong development and provide the learning techniques to make it possible. Where there is much rhetoric about lifelong education and the relevance of the community college curriculum, most continuing education programs rely heavily on traditional introductory courses or on what many teachers consider to be 'watered down' versions of 'college level' courses. There is much yet to be done in bringing the promise of lifelong learning into reality. [49, p. 72]

COMMUNITY SERVICES

Current Situation

Just as there has been a growing interest in adult evening and part-time education programs, there has also been a rise in the use of the community college as a conference center, as a place for community-oriented workshops, and as a meeting place for community organizations. The number of community-based advisory groups, many representing the special interests of local employers, minority groups, older age groups, etc., is expanding. The types and variety of services are almost as varied as the clientele to be served.

The response of community colleges to these multiple interests has been uneven. Prototype systems are beginning to emerge, however, which will serve as models for the future. A survey [71] of 100 randomly selected community colleges throughout the nation identified a basic set of programs that had been established at most institutions. This core effort included adult evening education programs and extension centers, the offering of noncredit courses and conferences and workshops to meet the needs of local citizens, a broadened spectrum of advisory groups, the use of college facilities by community organizations, the establishment of a full-time community service department within the college, and professional development of faculty and staff members involved in this aspect of the community college effort. This spectrum of community-oriented programs, rooted in past adult and continuing education services, should expand as community representatives become more articulate in their demand for such services.

Barriers and Constraints

Too often an initial commitment to community needs has been short-lived because the responsibility for the effort was lodged in one division in the community college. The marginal status of such a program has already been outlined in our discussion of the concern with adult and continuing education. A meaningful commitment on the part of community colleges to serving a wide spectrum of community needs requires the involvement of faculty, administrators, and even full-time students. Raines and Myran argue that the

entire college staff will need to develop increased interest and capacity to serve our new constituencies: senior citizens, ethnic minorities, women, low-income groups, handicapped persons, institutionalized persons, and so on. The community college is being challenged to move from its preoccupation with college-age students to a concern for lifelong learning. This concern will be expressed by serving the unique educational needs of members of constituencies who previously were given only marginal attention. Community involvement as an instrumentality for institutional and professional renewal is an idea whose time has come for the community college. [58]

To achieve these laudable objectives, the college's community service director must overcome a number of potential hazards or barriers. Offering noncredit courses flies in the face of a well-established tradition in all higher education—credit is the commodity which colleges sell to their potential consumers. It is also the criterion by which states offer support to their higher educational institutions. Once a consumer has accumulated a certain number of credits, he trades these in for a degree. The degree in turn determines his admissibility to a variety of careers. For those interested in college transfer, credit is still an unavoidable requirement. But for many adults and non-transfer-oriented students, credit courses arranged in semester sequence do not fill the bill. Alternatives are clearly needed, particularly when it comes to the determination of the amount of financial support to be offered to a college by the state.

We state in Chapter 6 that the wave of the future for community colleges will be to serve all adults, not just the traditional college-age student. Yet the community college seems destined to continue its fixation on the late adolescent. College presidents, administrators, and even state legislators must come to recognize that adults impose a different set of demands.

Another, not uncommon, institutional barrier to the development of improved community service programs is the tendency to continue the traditional offerings because few staff members are ready to accept new responsibilities. Changing community requirements may force role incumbents to adapt. Just as the hunted rabbit hopes to make himself less visible by standing motionless, so, too, do many faculty members when faced with the prospect of disrupting their "standard operating procedures." For this and other reasons, there is often a substantial lag between the emergence of a community need and an effective response to that need. The community service director can help to shorten that time lag, particularly if he supports innovative procedures designed to respond to community needs. We often find innovative approaches to instruction in the community service program which are later adapted or replicated by other departments of the college. This experimental potential of the community service program can be seriously hampered, however, by the lack of adequate resources or by resistance on the part of more conservative administrators within the larger organization.

Community service programs also enjoy a certain freedom in the selection of instructors, many of whom are recruited from the community. The fact that many are paid at an hourly rate and are nontenured makes it possible in some states to avoid the more stringent credential requirements laid down for full-time faculty members. This, of course, is a mixed blessing, since many of the community service program faculty are paid at a rate substantially below that of the full-time faculty members. The advantage is that the college can offer community service programs at a relatively low cost to participants. The disadvantage is that they may not be able to attract the best talent. Recent developments in collective bargaining may end or reduce this flexibility in hiring. Such an eventuality might well eliminate the extensive use of community resource persons, while the rise in salaries could price the community service programs out of the market.

Most community service efforts operate on a pay-as-you-go basis covered by fees charged to participants. A few states, such as California, Maryland, Florida, and Illinois, do have legislation providing state support for community service programs of a noncredit nature, but the majority of states do not. Federal funding, while providing some isolated and dramatic examples of the potential of community services, to date is an inadequate source of funds when measured against the need. We anticipate that more states will move in the direction of recognizing the legitimacy of community college expenditures in support of community-oriented services, but until that happens many community service programs will continue to operate on an uncertain financial footing.

Another obstacle blocking adults from full participation in community service programs involves the problems that they encounter when attempting to enroll or attend classes. The need for care of dependents, the lack of transportation, a sense of inadequacy in the learning situation, and inflexible work schedules—these are some of the factors that keep them from taking part. Supportive services should be provided by community colleges to assist adults in overcoming these obstacles. Day care centers, financial aid programs for adults, more accessible college facilities, corrective and remedial programs designed specifically for adults, and flexible scheduling represent just a few of the attempts to help adults overcome their practical or psychological handicaps.

Future Implications

Several important programs have evolved under the rubric of community services, each with a special mission. What follows is a description of these programs, which, if taken as a whole, might comprise a comprehensive community service model. In selecting these examples from among an array of possible services, the following three criteria were employed:

1 Would the program serve a common denominator of needs of various constituent groups in the community?
2 Would the service provide an opportunity for students and faculty to participate productively, both in terms of serving community needs and in terms of the participants' own personal development?
3 Would the response of the community college have a visible impact on or benefit to the community?

The examples which follow were taken from our field visits and from the work of the Kellogg Community Service Leadership Program of Michigan State University.

1. Community college resource institutes By 1980, community colleges will have established a variety of quasi-permanent institutes focused on community problems. These institutes will operate in cooperation with other community agencies or groups as nonprofit education corporations, addressing themselves to educationally related problems within the broad areas of concern such as unemployment, drug abuse, pollution, housing, etc. Such institutes would parallel the program suggested by the late A. A. Liverright in his vision of 1980, where colleges and universities would serve as effective community resources for adapting education to persistent and unresolved needs. We recommend that college-community resource institutes focus on clearly defined and critical community problems, with careful attention to community recommendations but not circumscribed by such recommendations. The proposed institutes should be structured on an ad hoc basis, with community-wide visibility, permanent staff and adjunct staff, reasonable autonomy, strong linkage to companion agencies, and a heavy focus on the educational implications of the problem under focus. Task-oriented teams of specialists supervised by a strong team leader capable of subordinating his own need for ego gratification would tackle community problems in a collaborative spirit.

Prototypes for such institutes are now in operation in a few locations. Lake Michigan College in Kalamazoo, Michigan, for example, sponsors an Institute for Professional and Paraprofessional Development. Participants from community agencies are being assisted with human relations problems that grow out of the effort to achieve fuller use of paraprofessionals in a community agency, civic government, or school setting.

The institute can also provide a desirable way of involving college faculty in the life of the community. Periodic sabbaticals should be provided to qualified faculty members so that they may work on a full-time basis in areas of related professional interest, such as pollution control, manpower development, or inner-city renewal. Not only should the institute provide for the involvement of qualified professionals as consultants on highly technical problems, but it should also serve as a much needed device for faculty renewal and student involvement in community affairs as it builds supportive educational programs and seeks to establish knowledge delivery systems. The institute might also serve as a recruitment mechanism whereby community personnel with particular skills could qualify as adjunct instructors at the college.

2. Community guidance centers By 1980, most community colleges will be operating community guidance centers which will assist adults in career planning, personal development, and educational planning. Such centers can and should be funded by city, county, or state agencies. Plans are being made at the present time to tie in local employment service offices with community college guidance centers, thus extending the range of services currently being provided by both types of organization.

A prototype of the community guidance center might be the Rockland County Guidance Center for Women, now in its fifth year of operation. It has provided career development counseling for approximately 400 clients per year and career information for another 2,000. The center was launched with special funds from the state of New York; however, after two years the center was forced to become self-sustaining through client fees supplemented by county appropriations. The budget of the Rockland Center averages about $60,000 per year.

3. Satellite learning centers Within the last two years, several new models for the provision of postsecondary learning opportunities have emerged. Cluster colleges, universities without walls, mini-colleges, SUNY's new Empire State College, Brookdale Community College's Central Campus Concept—they all represent ways of providing a college education without necessarily meeting in class-rooms or being physically located on a campus. The function of satellite learning centers will be to provide both credit and noncredit courses in storefront classrooms, through educational television, and in other ways which provide easier access for the potential student.

Several community colleges have moved in this direction already. Oakland Community College has established 28 off-campus centers enrolling approximately 4,000 students, many of whom claim they would not have gone to any of the three established campuses within the college district. Brookdale's program calls for the establishment of a central campus which contains only those essential facilities that are too costly to duplicate elsewhere in the district. Classrooms, libraries, and educational media will be located in off-campus facilities throughout the district. Laney Community College, one of several community colleges within the Peralta district, Oakland, California, sponsors two community service centers offering both vocational education and noncredit courses, such as a course in English as a Second Language. Rockland's mini-colleges offer special-purpose programs to small groups of students (100 or so) off campus. All are attempting to make educational opportunities more convenient and accessible.

4. Faculty renewal systems In the past, most programs for the updating and renewal of faculty members involved continued graduate work toward an advanced degree. While such planned study does qualify the successful candidate for administrative responsibilities and pay raises, it all too often proves to be of limited value in helping the faculty member to better understand and effectively relate to the needs of students and the community. An intimate knowledge of the ethnic backgrounds and life styles of students would facilitate the faculty's ability to develop curriculum outlines and adopt teaching strategies that are more relevant to the needs of their constituents. Since many community colleges are located in the middle of urban "laboratories" where a great deal of potential knowledge could be gleaned through involvement, faculty renewal programs can and will be programmed around providing opportunities for faculty members to become involved and to be of service.

Such a program will help to ensure that "action" research skills, consultant opportunities, and involvement in planned change efforts will aid immeasurably in strengthening and broadening the perspective of the faculty in their potential role in the community. A carefully structured reward system (graduate credit, reduced workload, travel) for participants will help to ensure that the return on the time invested by faculty is equal to the output.

5. Community information systems By focusing on identifying, collecting, processing, analyzing, and disseminating information

about the community, local community college staffs could come to understand the range and nature of the expectations of the various constituencies being served by the local college. Community needs and expectations would, in this fashion, be systematically reviewed for use by the college in its planning of future activities. Such "user-oriented" activities will help to ensure that the system is responsive to the concerns of the community. The various groups within the community will be encouraged to use this system in order to plan appropriate activities and to exploit whatever expertise might be available through the local institution.

6. Knowledge linkage systems One of the more challenging but potentially useful functions a community service program can perform would be serving as a linking pin between community groups and outside resource groups. University or industrial know-how will be effectively tied to "user" groups, with the staffs of community service centers serving as "extension agents." They will interpret the needs of the local community groups to potential consultants. Universities, various governmental agencies, industrialists, and consultants represent some of the potential resource groups who might be tapped.

The Human Resources Council in Montcalm County, Michigan, initiated through the leadership of the Community Services Department at Montcalm Community College, employed a part-time director who served as a coordinator for the various agencies, institutions, and other groups in the community devoted to community services. At Lake Michigan College in Benton Harbor, Michigan, the Southwestern Michigan Council for Continuing Education has been formed to coordinate and plan continuing and adult education programs on an areawide basis. The Kellogg Community Services Leadership Program at Michigan State University operates by means of close inter-college cooperation between three Michigan community colleges and the university. The four institutions jointly consider such matters as program development, administration, evaluation, research, and community problem solving. The consortium provides a ready-made means of bringing university and community college resources into the local community.

These six prototype programs, if put into practice on a broad scale, will do much to ensure a close and harmonious relationship between a college and its constituents. The reciprocal benefits to be derived—the community college staff discovering that it can be of service, the community resolving a chronic problem in a systematic manner—will provide the motivation that will eventually bring the two entities closer together.

CAREER EDUCATION

Current Situation

A wide variety of career education programs has emerged in recent years as the legitimate offering of the community college. Aided by recent legislation, career education at the postsecondary level is attracting increasing numbers of students who view it as an avenue for self-realization and economic security. The Vocational Education Act of 1963 and the amendments of 1968 helped to reorient the federal role in vocational education by recognizing the need to fund innovative programs which offered alternative pathways for preparing students, particularly disadvantaged students, for emerging occupations. A percentage of these funds was ear-marked for students at the postsecondary level.

How well the major objectives of this landmark legislation have been served nationally is difficult to assess. The existing federal information system from which national data are extracted was designed originally to monitor how well states succeeded in meeting the requirements of the federal legislation. Definitions of what constitute vocational enrollments vary dramatically from state to state. Common criteria for determining who are the disadvantaged, adult, and part-time students are also lacking. Little is known about the characteristics of part-time students enrolled in career education programs and about the quality of the learning experience available to them. What we do know is that postsecondary career education programs are expanding and expanding fast.

Barriers and Constraints

Improved instructional strategies for career education, while they have received a good deal of attention, have yet to be widely accepted. Because of the long tradition of federal aid for vocational education, dating back to 1917, many of the programs and practices established then have continued to command the lion's share of the federal appropriation. More recently, the expansion of federal support for R&D in vocational education has accelerated the pace of experimentation.

Continued support for vocational education over the years has also enabled the state directors of vocational education programs to build a strong political base among key state legislators and officials. The comparatively recent arrival of state community college directors has made it more difficult for them to line up political support among state legislators for consideration when career education funds are allocated. Because much of the past effort in vocational education has been concentrated at the secondary school level, some state directors of vocational education have been reluctant to endorse or support the expansion of postsecondary vocational education in other than area vocational schools, institutions which happen to be under their direct control.

Moving from the state to the local level, one of the major goals of public community colleges has been to aid adults and older adolescents in their preparation for employment. Responsiveness to local labor-market opportunities has been aided by the extensive use of advisory committees made up of employers and union representatives from the local community. Unions have traditionally depended upon the occupational training opportunities offered to their members by the community college. Adults have evidenced their enthusiasm for postsecondary programs by their continued willingness to enroll in both day and evening courses. The success of graduates from community college career education programs has been documented by a number of recent follow-up studies. [60] Why the concern, then, with this area of activity?

Our study findings show that career education within the community college setting is experiencing difficulties. In the chapter on faculty characteristics, we analyzed the attitudes of the liberal arts faculty, many of whom see little value in providing a career training option to students. This point of view, together with substantive problems encountered when attempts are made to merge the liberal arts curriculum with the occupational curriculum, has resulted in few effectively articulated curriculum offerings of cluster courses. While there tends to be wide-spread interest among the career education faculty in the concept of an "organic curriculum" which combines the need to develop intellectual skills with those required for entry into an occupation, examples of a successful melding process are difficult to find. Where faculty teams composed of specialists from various disciplines have been able to integrate their program objectives into a unified curriculum plan, positive results have been achieved. [5] But team planning requires a high order of human relations skills and a willingness to subordinate departmental or diciplinary interests to the larger interest. Few faculty members have been trained to plan and work with representatives of other disciplines.

Not only are there problems of horizontal articulation and collaboration within an institution, but communication links with other institutions purporting to offer career education programs to local residents are lacking. There are very few reasons why a high school principal or the director of an area vocational school should not collaborate with the department chairman or dean of career education located at a nearby community college, but state and district administrative structures militate against such cooperation. Because of the relative autonomy from the local tax support base enjoyed by vocational education, vocational high school and area vocational school directors can, if they choose, "go it alone" in deciding what courses to offer. Duplicate offerings and nonarticulated courses at high school and community college levels are the result.

While the high cost of poor articulation and duplicate offerings within some communities underscores the need for improved interinstitutional communication, there is growing evidence that vocational education as a discipline has not kept pace with the requirements of a computer-based, postindustrial society. The rise in service occupations, for example, has put a premium on communication skills (writing, listening, speaking, and reading skills), which were not as much in demand during an earlier era with a production-oriented society. Interpersonal or human relations skills required to establish and maintain open and effective communication with customers must now be acquired through channels other than those provided by the public schools. Unfortunately, even some graduates of certificate or associate degree programs can be described as not having achieved an adequate level of verbal fluency. Many carry with them a dislike of learning which will hinder or reduce their motivation to continue their learning beyond their formal years of education. What should have been the joy of discovery and personal achievement has been replaced, for many, by disillusionment and frustration.

Students as well as faculty continue to think of the career or terminal degree program as something quite different from the college parallel program. A majority of students, uncertain with regard to their future career interests, pursue the college parallel program because they have some vague notion that they will want to transfer to a four-year institution at a later date. Their perceptions are distorted by status needs and the expectation of heightened mobility. Even those with definite career interests will sometimes shy away from career programs for the same reasons. Since only one-third of this group eventually transfers to a four-year institution, the remainder either drop out or settle for an associate degree without qualifying for a career. Those hoping to enroll in the college parallel program at a later date soon discover that it is difficult to transfer without taking a number of additional credits. Because of the sometimes narrowly focused career education curricula and the attitudes of university and college registrars toward career education programs, those who wish to make the change are severely handicapped.

Past attempts to improve career education programs at the postsecondary level have tended to deal with fragmented pieces of the learning system. Those responsible for implementing improvements are beginning to recognize that each subsystem or part of the learning experience must be viewed within the total context of the college environment. Unless career education reforms are undertaken with the total system in mind, attempted changes in one or two areas will be short-term demonstrations at best.

Future Implications

As a result of growing dissatisfaction, traditional career education programs, where the emphasis is put upon lectures and "canned" films and filmstrips, will give ground to programs centering on individualized education. The following five examples of emerging approaches offer new alternatives for resolving the more important issues in postsecondary career education.

1. Matching students with jobs The demand for skilled workers seldom develops independently of the existing labor market and institutional arrangements for training. Acceptance of graduates from a program designed to train teacher aides, for example, requires close coordination with potential employers. Setting up realistic licensing and credentialing requirements (and dealing with the potential opposition from those with whom such responsibilities are already lodged) will require the full cooperation and collaboration of those who will serve as gatekeepers.

The ability to provide students, guidance counselors, and curriculum planners with detailed job information and skill requirements will make it possible not only to keep training programs current and relevant, but also to aid students in making appropriate career choices. Martin Katz and E.T.S., in conjunction with Mercer County Community College, Trenton, N.J., [41] have designed a computer-based guidance system which enables students and counselors to readily obtain career information in a form such that students can estimate their own chance of success in a given occupational field.

The students are given the opportunity to test the efficacy of their more closely held values by assuming various career roles and observing how their values conflict with the value systems commonly associated with those occupations. (By means of this computer-simulated career experience, students are helped to evaluate their hierarchy of values in terms of the compatibility of such values with those most often found in selected career areas.) This computer-based System of Interactive Guidance and Information (SIGI) will eventually serve several institutions within the Trenton metropolitan area, linked together by means of leased telephone lines. The major barrier to participation by institutions outside the Trenton area would be the cost of the leasing charges associated with a telephone hookup.

The College of DuPage in Illinois now provides a Computer Vocational Information System (CVIS) for nearby Willowbrook High School [22] as well as for its own students. This individualized vocational information system provides both students and counselors with on-line access to career information. Off-line reports of student interaction with the computer are also available for use by counselors. The high school students in the area are able to ascertain what nearby colleges and vocational learning opportunities are available, together with possible sources of scholarship aid. Information on local employment opportunities is also stored and retrieved by means of the computer. The students are given access to all information pertaining to their advancement as well as their own achievement and aptitude test results. Tests are interpreted for the student by the computer, and it provides them with the opportunity to compare their own scores with those of various normative groups.

G. Brian Jones of the American Institute for Research has been working closely with Foothill College in California to design a guidance system which enables the student to make more realistic career choices and career plans, starting with an intensive needs assessment effort. The student is given a deck of cards to sort, each card containing a particular goal. The resulting goal hierarchy is reviewed by a counselor, who then helps the student lay out an appropriate sequence of learning opportunities around the individual student's needs inventory.

2. Faculty training Pre- and in-service training for those in the technical and vocational fields is different from the training which those who teach the liberal arts and general education courses receive. While a master's degree is often a minimum requirement for the latter faculty, there is considerably more latitude given to those in the career education field in terms of accepting work experience as the equivalent of graduate work. Many consider this practice to be one of the strengths of community colleges because of the flexibility it offers in faculty recruitment; however, it does tend to intensify the split between those in academic programs and those teaching nonacademic courses. Our interviews with faculty representatives lead us to conclude that cooperation between the various faculty groups would be enhanced if such groups were given the opportunity to share in a common preservice training experience which emphasized the unique goals and functions of community junior colleges. By building a common identity for all faculty members through exposure to a core program of this type during preservice training, better understanding and cooperation between academic and nonacademic instructors would be achieved.

A number of dramatic efforts in teacher training aimed specifically at preparing new faculty for teaching roles in junior colleges are now under way. The Union for Research and Experimentation in Higher Education, located on the campus at Antioch College, in cooperation with five teacher-training institutions, has designed a master's degree program [24] for preparing community college instructors. Graduates of this program are expected to complete five or six years of training (including two years of undergraduate work at a junior college) combining, by means of cooperative education, intern experience with individualized learning opportunities while in training.

Eastern Washington State College has designed a preservice faculty training program for technical faculty members based on the concept of developing the ability to counsel students as well as mastering an occupational specialty. Effective teaching skills are developed around internship experience, a thorough knowledge of instructional techniques, familiarity with various media, and an understanding of the learning problems of students with widely varying educational capacities and interests.

3. Individualizing instruction and career education While considerable attention has been given to designing individualized instructional procedures for junior college students of varying ability levels and

learning styles, the full impact of such procedures on occupational education programs has yet to be felt. Effective exploitation of this concept by the career education faculty member will require a raft of new teaching materials and administrative procedures, as well as profound changes in attitude. The faculty member will take on new responsibilities, such as evaluating individual student progress, prescribing learning sequences, testing, and repeating this same cycle as the student moves from one level of skill to another.

The Naval Academy in Annapolis, Maryland, has demonstrated the feasibility of self-study and multimedia programs in occupational education. It has successfully field-tested a computer-managed instructional system in three subject areas covering the freshman year at the academy. Two of the three courses are vocational in orientation.

Oakland Community College, near Detroit, Michigan, has been attempting to personalize its learning process, tailoring its curriculum to individual student learning styles by working with students to develop a personalized plan of study for each. Graduates of the applied sciences and arts program are expected not only to qualify for work in one of seven broad occupational clusters but also to have established a sound base for continuing their formal education toward a four-year college degree if they elect to do so. Each student is expected to develop an individualized plan of study with the aid of a battery of diagnostic tests and counseling. Through a process of "cognitive style mapping," a team of teachers and a student jointly prepare a personalized study plan geared to accommodate and exploit the student's strengths and weaknesses. A computer is used to keep track of each individual student's progress. [53]

The multimedia instructional system at Mt. San Jacinto College in California has built its programs around the careful specification of instructional objectives so that individual study, small group sessions, large groups, and lab sessions can be fully exploited. Students obtain much of their lecture material and instruction from taped lessons and worksheets. They are permitted to proceed at their own rate of speed and receive credit when it is earned. The instructor serves as a consultant and diagnostician ready to provide assistance when needed.

4. **Simulation and troubleshooting** Perhaps of greatest use to the career educator and the vocational guidance counselor will be simulation games and equipment. Career games, introduced and developed by such pioneers as Sarane Boocock [9] and John

Krumboltz, [43] have gained widespread acceptance among vocational guidance counselors and others concerned with helping students make appropriate career choices. Boocock's "Life Career" game is designed to assist students in thinking through the implications of alternative choices available to them at various times during late adolescence and adulthood. Krumboltz's problem-solving experiences simulate career exploration by enabling the participant to try typical chores associated with a given profession or occupation. Following an hour or so of simulated work in accounting, for example, a prospective trainee might be induced to pursue a career in that particular occupation. If not, he'll be just that much more experienced for having tried at least a sample of the accountant's work.

In previous years, most of the training equipment employed by vocational educators simply duplicated the tools and machinery an employee would be expected to know how to operate on the job. Because much of this "on-line" equipment is not designed for instructional purposes and often fails to take into account such considerations as safety, costs, or space restrictions, it is not well suited for the classroom. Simulated equipment offers training experience under similar operating conditions at a considerably lower cost. Often the simplicity of the equipment makes it easier for the instructor to train the student in the basic skills, with high transfer potential of what they have learned to actual production equipment in a relatively short time.

Among the newer instructional procedures to be employed in career education is the use of a small computer to simulate defects in a troubleshooting exercise. The student is required to make systematic tests using a schematic diagram in order to find the cause of improper equipment performance. As a learner develops his diagnostic skills, the difficulty involved in finding the defect can be increased. A large variety of diagnostic exercises can be provided through this simulation approach.

5. Articulated tracking A few institutions are redefining the requirements for both the career and the college transfer programs. The career program students are given credits which closely parallel those required for college transfer. Many students in the career program who will want further study beyond the two-year level at some future date will be able to acquire it if their achievements have been properly accredited. Core curricula which crosscut departmental specialties are being designed. Individual guidance is being provided so that each student is better able to make an intelligent

choice before entering a particular career program. Students who have an interest, for example, in the applied arts are encouraged to take courses in the humanities and social sciences in order to help them achieve greater insight into their career field. Cooperative education (coordinated work/study programs) is offered as an integral part of the curriculum. Off-campus experience adds the needed dimension of providing job training and exposure to a variety of possible working environments.

Perhaps the best curriculum plan yet devised for community college students was outlined by Norman C. Harris at an AACJC conference on occupational education. A comprehensive junior college should "take students where they are and prepare them for their next goal in life—be it matriculation at the state university or caring for the sick in the general hospital. All students on the campus are college students, and curriculum planning should reflect this philosophy. All occupational education curricula should present a carefully balanced mix of general and liberal arts education, theory and technical support courses, and specialized skill courses." [34, p. 46] Harris proposes that beginning students in a community college should move in either of two directions. Fully qualified students would move immediately into general education and basic core subjects. Those with certain deficiencies would move into a one-semester or longer developmental program. In a typical curriculum plan, five core areas would be provided for those working toward an associate degree in occupational education: (1) a general education core, including courses in English, humanities, political science, etc.; (2) a basic core in engineering technology and industrial technology; (3) a basic core in business programs; (4) a basic core in health programs; and (5) a basic core in public service programs. Each of the occupationally related cores would offer specialized courses in the chosen field of technology after about 20 credit hours in the basic core curriculum. Graduates would receive an associate degree in their selected field, e.g., electronic technology, data processing, dental technology, law enforcement. Harris's concluding comments are as appropriate today as they were in 1966.

We cannot continue to put three-fourths of our junior college educational effort on the needs of one-fourth of the students. Middle-level youth in junior colleges outnumber "superior" youth by 3 to 1. It is high time that we stopped neglecting their educational needs—high time that we stopped regarding occupational education as somehow being not respectable. The needs of average students are also the nation's needs in this era of change. The junior college can serve all of its students and the nation in the decades ahead. It is our challenge to see that it serves both well. [34, p. 47]

DEVELOPMENTAL EDUCATIONAL PROGRAMS

Current Situation

The challenge of the open-door college can most often be dramatically witnessed in the classroom. The heterogeneity of student backgrounds and ability levels forces many a faculty member to reexamine his traditional teaching methods and to work with each student in whatever way is effective. Literally millions of dollars and untold man-hours of effort have been invested in diagnosing and prescribing compensatory learning programs for those students who, based upon their normative test scores, are judged unlikely to handle college-level requirements successfully. Every community junior college counselor knows the limitations of such predictions, particularly when applied to students from disadvantaged backgrounds. Helping to see that such predictions do not come true has become the responsibility of a special breed of educator, those in charge of the remedial education programs.

The old concept of remediation implied that something had to be done to the student to make him eligible for entry into a college program. The modern student development programs are designed to assist students in acquiring those skills and attitudes needed to achieve their unique goals and aspirations on their own terms. The advent of Bloom's concept of mastery [7] has brought with it a shift away from an emphasis on making a student eligible for entry into a program toward an emphasis on helping him achieve whatever goals he may commit himself to at his own rate and in his own way. The term "developmental education" will be used in this analysis, rather than the more limited term "remedial education," in order to encompass the broader program of helping students determine where they are and where they want to be.

Community junior colleges, unlike their four-year counterparts, strive to accommodate all applicants, whether overachievers or underachievers. A fair number of these students lack confidence in themselves and the necessary learning skills to cope with college. Many have unrealistic aspirations, making them candidates for special counseling. Compensatory or developmental programs attempt to satisfy aspirations by moving beyond the conventional statement that low achievers do not have the ability to measure up. Such efforts start with the assumption that all (or most) students have the ability to achieve under the right circumstances. Standardized tests calibrated for large groups of middle-class whites have little utility when administered to urban blacks. The disadvantaged student, for example, who failed to develop adequate reading and communications skills in high school and who carries with him the scars from his earlier encounters reacts in quite a different manner to the competitive environment of the college classroom than do students with well-developed verbal skills. What the low achiever needs is someone with whom he can identify on an emotional level, experiencing a sense of acceptance and concern, rather than admonitions to match or exceed a nonrelevant set of performance standards.

A recently completed study at Miami-Dade Junior College [46] reported that first-time college students who scored below the twenty-first percentile on the verbal section of the SCAT test were also in need of some form of intensive psychological counseling. Most suffered from lack of confidence, shyness, and an inability to work with authority figures. The report observed that the emotional problems of the low achiever were as significant as his poorly developed learning skills. Coping with such problems requires a system which reinforces in a positive way the student's sense of self-worth and at the same time provides him with an opportunity to develop his intellectual abilities. How to design and install developmental programs that handle such diverse needs requires a body of well-tested procedures. Very few now exist, but those that do are well worth describing. Before these promising examples are outlined, however, some attention needs to be given to the reasons why others have not succeeded.

Barriers and Constraints

Even though the concern for the low achiever in community junior colleges dates back almost to World War II, empirical evidence of successful programs which meet the needs of such students is noteworthy by its absence. Roueche, [59] after a thorough review of the literature on the topic, concluded that little effort has been made to evaluate the effectiveness of these programs. What evidence there is, together with the findings of Project Focus, reveals the following problems.

Most community junior college faculty are ill-prepared to handle the underachieving or low-aptitude student. Those selected for the job frequently enjoy low seniority and no tenure. Such assignments reflect the fact that teaching a remedial course is a low-prestige assignment. (There are notable exceptions to this practice, and they will be cited later.) The inexperienced faculty member, often fresh out of graduate school, has had little in the way of orientation or training in coping with the special needs of this group of students. Too few resources and inappropriate instructional materials conspire to defeat even the most conscientious instructor. The absence of alternative ways of linking students with tutors, faculty with students, and students with students fuels the fires of frustration.

Not only do faculty members often feel unprepared and inadequate to meet the needs of the special student, but the objectives for developmental programs are often vague and sometimes contradictory. Whether developmental programs are expected to salvage the student and provide him with a second chance, "cool out" the student, or serve a custodial function has yet to be determined in many institutions. Goal clarification would enhance the probability that students assigned to developmental programs would perceive them as potentially beneficial experiences rather than as ones to be avoided.

Many low-achieving students come from families where there has been limited contact with higher education and little encouragement to pursue a college degree. Since such families place greater value upon their off-spring's earning ability, they encourage them to find employment immediately after high school. College attendance, they feel, demands financial means beyond the capability of the family. In short, there is little reason for students from such backgrounds to aspire to or understand what college has to offer. Those who do enroll often do so with the idea that college will advance their career mobility more rapidly than work experience. Unrealistic aspirations coupled with uncertainty make such students less apt to persist in their efforts when confronted with learning difficulties.

Students are assigned to developmental programs primarily on the basis of their verbal skills as assessed by standardized achievement tests and previous record. If a student falls below a certain cut-off point on a curve, he is automatically assigned to the special aid program. Unfortunately, below-average performance also implies that the student is inferior. How valid these criteria are when applied to those reared in an urban environment who speak the language of their own subculture has been a legitimate point of contention among minority groups for the past decade. Malcolm X Community College, for example, refuses to use the word "remediation" when dealing with low achievers and attempts to work with the student where he "is," based on his unique set of qualifications and level of development. By avoiding some of the stereotypes associated with poorly developed verbal skills, Malcolm X College is charting individually tailored development programs for all its students.

Standardized achievement test scores have been found to be poor predictors of a student's performance in occupational education programs. Measures of verbal ability do not help predict the student's manipulative abilities. Nor do achievement tests measure the psychological dimensions of the student. The underachieving student often lacks confidence and is emotionally unprepared to cope with a community college environment. The inability to handle test situations effectively and to relate to authority figures also conspires against the student who has been told over and over again that he does not measure up.

Due to the increasing pressures on two-year colleges to accept all students who apply for admission and to the belief that a college degree is a passport to the future, low-achieving students are entering community junior colleges at an accelerating rate. Chapter 3's report on students', faculty, and presidents' perceptions of goals demonstrates that there is an increasing sense of commitment to effectively serving this segment of the society. Roueche sums up the issue when he states:

"With pressures from society to lengthen the educational experience of all students, the low-achieving student has become conspicuous in community colleges. No semantical niceties will cover or hide the issue. No matter what the student is called, his problem is the same. To the extent that community-junior colleges can identify these students and provide meaningful educational experiences for them, the institution has implemented the concept of the open door." [59, p. 15]

Future Implications

The low-achieving student has been handled in one of three ways by most community junior colleges. The first is to assign him to a required series of remedial courses, a practice we have already examined. The second is to provide a variety of special services, such as tutoring, intensive counseling, and individualized study. The third approach attempts to modify the administrative support structure in order to facilitate the continued enrollment of such students in the hope that they will eventually improve. Modification of registration and grading procedures and the accommodation of students on probation are the most familiar administrative adjustments.

These strategies have been only partially successful because they have not attempted to deal with the student on his own terms in the total learning environment. What follows is an idealized approach pieced together from observations made during visits to a number of innovative institutions throughout the course of the study. Where specific examples suit the situation, they are offered, but this should in no way be construed as an exhaustive inventory of ongoing programs.

Tomorrow's institutions will select their most able instructors to work with the low-achieving student. As learning specialists, they will enjoy a certain status and have administrative backing for their efforts. The training of these learning specialists will help them understand and accept the idea that all students can achieve, but that not all students are predisposed to a verbally oriented instructional mode. This select group of instructors will be chosen because of their student-centeredness rather than because of their institutional orientation or departmental identification.

Miami-Dade Junior College has recently established an experimental program for the low-achieving student which involves small groups of no more than eight students linked with a carefully selected, well-trained instructor or group leader. These close-knit groups are purposely structured to ensure close student and faculty involvement with each other. If, for example, a student should fail to show up for a class on a given day, one or two of the other students and frequently the instructor will drop by after class to see what happened. Financial aid problems are quickly remedied through a special fund that the instructors are permitted to tap for emergency purposes. The sense of closeness and group identity aimed for in these small primary groups reinforces the individual's commitment and his feeling of rapport with the group.

In addition, the North Campus of Miami-Dade has set up a small Office of Staff and Organizational Development (OSOD) specifically aimed at assisting individual faculty members in establishing new instructional procedures and experimental courses which deal more effectively with the "new" student. A group of internal consultants is used to facilitate faculty training and development along the lines just described. While the role of OSOD extends beyond improving the staff's capability for working with low achievers, this has been one of its primary areas of concern to date. It hopes to introduce a variety of tested innovations which will motivate the faculty to work more effectively with students on an individual basis. The traditional instructional patterns of the past are being replaced by more flexible learning opportunities designed to accommodate individual student learning styles.

Perhaps even more important than finding and training competent staff members and building a climate of concern for the student is a recognition of the need for individualizing counseling and learning experiences. By accepting the student where he is at the time he enters a community junior college and putting him in situations where he can succeed, we will do much to ensure optimal progress. By considering the total student, his self-concept, his motives, his learning styles, his strengths and weaknesses, trained counselors can help each student determine his own plan for advancement.

Instructional technology will be employed to assist faculty members and students alike in adapting learning materials and procedures to individual differences. Such technology will aid administrators in allocating time, staff, and resources more efficiently to achieve more clearly specified goals and objectives. Career training through television, computer-aided instruction, and programed instruction are just a few of the ways that are being adopted to improve student learning rates and abilities. The faculty member in such programs will be at the heart of the system but will also take on new responsibilities. As a learning manager, he will diagnose abilities and prescribe learning sequences tailored to individual needs. He will need to maintain an up-to-date awareness of new instructional materials. Such materials will include those aimed at strengthening the student's career awareness, citizenship responsibilities, societal values, and sense of self-awareness and personal worth.

Compton Community College in California has designed a program that seeks to determine a student's level of achievement, identify his strengths and weaknesses, and then put him into learning situations where he can become a complete person. Successes are the rule, not the exception. Few students are put on scholastic probation. Career education students are encouraged to take general education programs and vice versa. Most important, counselors help students arrange flexible programs of study designed to achieve the student's educational objectives, not those of the institution.

Institutions such as Contra Costa Community College are providing low achievers with the opportunity to work closely with tutors (many recruited from student ranks) on a one-to-one basis. Such tutors are trained to look upon every student as a worthwhile person with unique capabilities. It is up to the tutor to assist in discovering these sometimes hidden characteristics and allowing him to flourish and grow. The assumption is that in the tutoring situation the student will feel free to ask questions and to review materials without the fear of slowing down the rest of the class. Learning acquires a new dimension when a close personal relationship develops with the tutor.

Involvement of the student in more intimate group relationships, tutoring on a one-to-one basis, and recognizing the needs of the total student help the low achiever begin to view the instructional program as a rewarding one. As essentially negative perceptions are replaced with favorable ones through positive reinforcement and support, students will be less likely to avoid or withdraw from such programs. Improving the student's self-concept and helping him to establish more realistic aspirations are as important to the low achiever as improving his basic learning skills.

To sum up these observations on the direction in which developmental education programs ought to be moving, one could hardly improve upon the statement made in a report to the Junior College Division of the Texas College and University System by its Compensatory Education Project. [21] It begins with the recognition that motivation is the key to the high failure rate among disadvantaged students. "The most promising solution to this problem . . . is a motivational program in which students are given a taste of success, helped to develop some self-respect, helped to develop realistic and attainable career objectives, helped to feel they belong at the community college, and helped to develop skills in reading and communication." The proposed Texas program will start with those areas in which the students can do well. It then hopes to provide new skills, recognizing that frequently the people who can help the most are faculty members from similar ethnic backgrounds or other students of like orientation. Failure experiences are avoided, including massive testing programs. They recommend that the use of rigid cutoff scores on a single placement test be discontinued and that a student's past record, his motivation, and his native ability (as determined by culturally unbiased test measures) be used for placement and evaluation purposes. In this way, the educationally handicapped, the minority, and the low-achieving student is helped to feel that he belongs and that there is a person or a group with whom he can identify in a primary-group fashion.

Chapter 6.
The
Pragmatic 70s

The United States is well embarked upon what may be appropriately described as the "pragmatic 70s." According to Drucker, [25] we are entering a decade of relative stability, with the free-spending, free-living teenagers of the 1960s becoming the serious, job-seeking young adults of the 1970s. Such a shift reflects the dramatic move, in a few short years, of our population gravity center from late adolescence to early adulthood. The wave of war babies is about to crash against the shore of a tightening labor market.

The shock that young adults will experience upon entering an overcrowded labor market will be strong. During the decade, 40 percent more people will be seeking jobs each year than in the previous year. Thirty-four million young adults will be entering the labor market for the first time. These war babies of the late 1940s and early 1950s have just begun to enter today's labor market in large numbers, many of them doing so after taking a few years out for college, military service, or travel. Since half of our males and about two-fifths of our females elected to go to college during the latter part of the 1960s, the full impact of this group on the labor market is just beginning to be felt.

These aspiring workers will glut the labor market, creating a condition of forced leisure for those in the lower- and middle-level occupations. Too few jobs to go around will motivate both unions and employers to shorten the work week, discourage moonlighting, spread the work load, and, in the process, enhance the number of leisure hours.

Work and leisure may well become the primary concerns of the modern generation. Chart 6-1 shows the percentage of population growth by age groups through 1980. Note that the age groups 20-24 and 25-34 will show the most dramatic increases during the decade. Those falling into these age brackets, we predict, represent the most significant enrollment growth potential for community colleges precisely because of their need for occupational preparation and retraining. The upward shift in the average age of full- and part-time students already reflects a move in this direction. Accommodating the needs and expectations of an older, more self-directed, and more highly motivated student body will require major adjustments in teaching methods, faculty attitudes, course scheduling, organization, and prerequisites for enrollment—in short, in all those courses, procedures, and traditional practices which were geared to the youthful expectations of the traditional (19–20-year-old) college-age student.

Current trends suggest that during this decade there will be a *lessening* in the demand for a traditional college education and a rising demand for career education, a large part of which will be at the postsecondary level. The Carnegie Commission on Higher Education reports a "go-stop-go" situation between now and the year 2000, with overall enrollments in higher education expanding at a considerably reduced rate during the 1970s (as contrasted with a doubling of enrollments during the 1960s), not expanding during the period 1980-1990, and again increasing, this time by one-third, during the 1990s. These predictions are based upon several assumptions, e.g., that approximately 50 percent of the "college-age" population will be enrolled at any one time. The Carnegie Commission [16] predicts that enrollments will grow more in accord with societal growth during this and the following two decades, in contrast to their rate of growth during the last century, when enrollment doubled every 14 to 15 years. This projection, coupled with our own observation of population trends, lends credence to the prediction that nontraditional students—those over 21, many married and working full time—may well account for much of the enrollment increase within public community colleges during this decade.

By 1980, the Bureau of Labor Statistics [11] predicts, there will be slightly more than 100 million gainfully employed workers (see Chart 6.2). More workers will be coming into the labor force (41

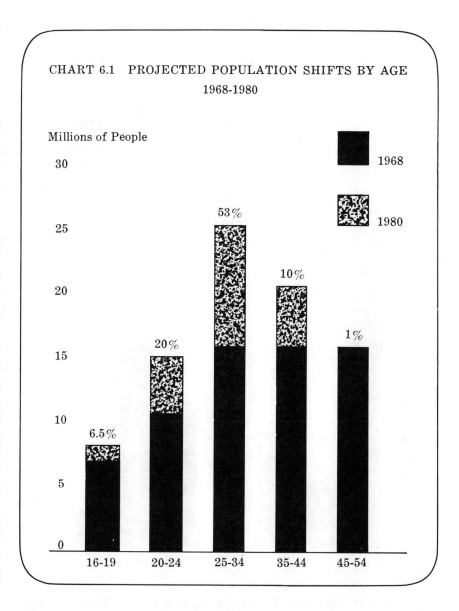

CHART 6.1   PROJECTED POPULATION SHIFTS BY AGE
1968-1980

Millions of People

million) than will be leaving it (26 million). Of those coming in, 34 million will be new, young workers looking for their first jobs, 6 million will be women who delayed working because of their children, and 1 million will be immigrants. To qualify for the more appealing and remunerative careers, many of these new workers will

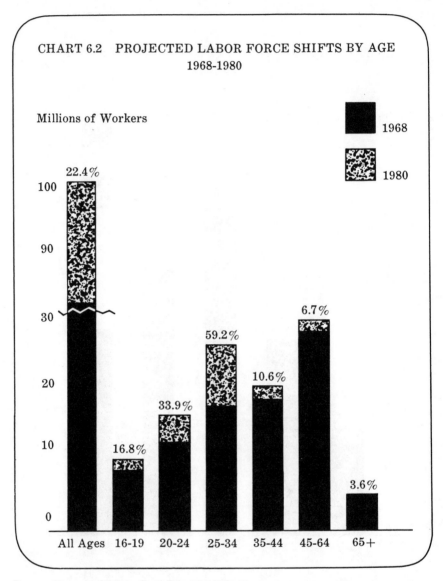

CHART 6.2   PROJECTED LABOR FORCE SHIFTS BY AGE
1968-1980

Millions of Workers

1968

1980

Source: Bureau of Labor Statistics, *The U.S. Economy in 1980* (Washington, D.C.: U.S. Department of Labor. Bulletin 1973, 1970).

require training at a postsecondary level. Others already in the labor force will seek to enhance their earning power and position through retraining and upgrading of existing skills.

Just what effect the increased number of young adults and women participating in the labor market will have on the number of adults seeking job preparation or retraining is difficult to predict. Our data indicate that 50 percent of the students attending college full time are working 15 hours or more a week. The median age for part-time students is 27 and rising. Increased leisure time and more flexible course scheduling, not to mention the dispersal of learning activities into offices and homes, will make it increasingly possible for adults to participate in college-level courses while continuing to work.

The number of 25- to 34-year-olds in the labor force will grow by almost 60 percent during the 1970s. One out of every four workers, 26 million in all, will fall into this age group by 1980. Increased job competition will force many to reconsider their career goals and seek out more viable opportunities. The more talented and ambitious will be able to fill slots now reserved for those midway in their careers (35 to 44), both because of changing job requirements and the difficulty some older workers will have in adapting and because of the short supply of workers in this older age category. Replacement of older by younger workers will, to some extent, be a result of the higher level of education attained by the younger workers. This fact may serve as a spur to mid-careerists to increase their participation in part-time training and educational programs. Those with higher levels of education (and better-developed learning skills) will fare better than those without.

The continued rise in the number of high school graduates and persons attending college not only will raise the overall educational attainment level of the nation's labor force but will also tend to raise the job entry requirements, making a two- or four-year college degree mandatory for occupations once requiring lower levels of education. There is also the complicating factor of a predicted oversupply of engineers and teachers, now in training in four-year college programs. Just what effect they will have on the market for paraprofessionals in these areas is difficult to predict. Chart 6.3 projects the number of job openings by occupation through 1980 in selected fields. What may appear to be ample opportunities for employment in these areas can of course be distorted by employer requirements which favor college graduates, whether two- or four-year degree holders. The outlook for those with associate degrees continues to be good. One of the more salient reports from the Bureau of Labor Statistics, entitled "College Educated Workers, 1968-1980," [10] comments that the "extensive network of community and junior colleges in the United States has been beneficial in many ways." It cites institutional flexibility and responsiveness to local manpower needs as definite plus factors. Students from low-income families and

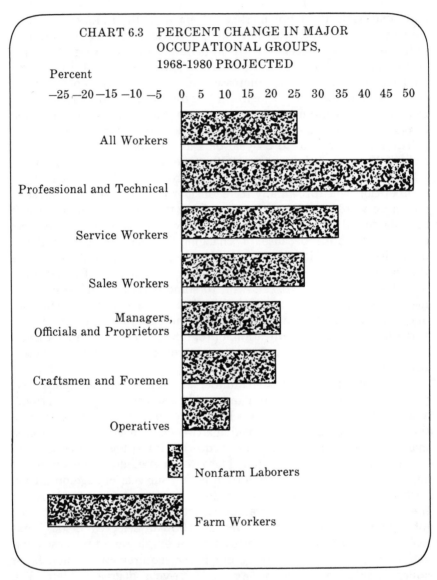

Source: Bureau of Labor Statistics, *Occupational Manpower and Training Needs* (Washington, D.C.: U.S. Department of Labor, Bulletin 1701).

others who could not afford college are now able to attend. In 1964, according to this report, about 34 percent of all two-year college students (full- and part-time) were in career training programs. In 1968, the number of career students had increased to 40 percent. Our data indicate that approximately 25 percent of the full-time students enrolled in the spring of 1971 were pursuing a career education degree or certificate. While job placement information has been scarce, two recent studies [24, 48] demonstrate that associate degree holders find jobs more quickly, are better paid, and advance more rapidly than graduates of technical institutes or high school-level vocational programs. The Godfrey and Holmstrom study revealed that 80 percent of the two-year college students graduating with an associate degree in 1967 went on to enroll in additional educational programs on a full- or part-time basis. A third of this group received their bachelor's degree two years later. Those who elected to go to work immediately following graduation from the two-year college were earning substantially more than the median wage for all 20- to 24-year-olds in 1969. Associate degree holders, according to the Somers and Fernbach study, advanced more rapidly than technical institute graduates, with an average rate of return of 14 percent on the investment.[1]

EMERGING EMPLOYMENT OPPORTUNITIES

Many job categories requiring technical-level skills are expected to expand during the 1970s. Student interest in career education programs at the postsecondary level will continue its upward trend, reflecting an upsurge in demand for clerical workers, technicians, service workers, and proprietors of small business enterprises. Clerical occupations alone are expected to expand by 35 percent, from 12.8 million in 1968 to 17.3 million in 1980. The demand for technicians in the engineering and science fields and in the health service occupations will expand by roughly 61 percent. This figure does not include some of the newer occupations, such as social work aides, marine technologists, and environmental technicians.

The increased demand for engineering and science technicians and draftsmen reflects the increasing complexity of modern technology

---

[1] The controversy surrounding just what benefits college graduates derive from their investment in a postsecondary education is not easily resolved. Hanson and Whitmer, speaking at the American Council on Education's 54th Annual Meeting, argued that the rate of return on the investment for two years of college does not exceed 10 percent. While they do not cite any recent studies directed at A.A. degree graduates, they make the unwarranted assumption that the individual rate of return for a student completing one to three years of college is the same as for a student completing a two-year program of study. Clearly the two references cited above represent more focused assessments. The problem of the comparability of various populations of students, e.g., technical institute graduates and community college graduates, opens to question the validity of the findings of a number of cost-benefit studies of the type described.

TABLE 6.1   Employment opportunities by selected occupations, 1968 and
projected 1980 requirements

Selected occupations	Employment in 1968	Projected 1980 requirements	Percent growth	Annual openings
Engineering and science technicians and draftsmen	915,000	1,325,000	45	46,300
Dental hygienists	16,000	33,500	109	2,400
Library technicians	70,000	125,000	77	9,000
Police officers	285,000	360,000	27	15,000

Source: U.S. Department of Labor, Bureau of Labor Statistics, *Occupational
Manpower and Training Needs*, Bulletin 1701, Washington, D.C.

in the private sector. Production planning, technical sales, continued
emphasis on automation of the industrial process, and the growth of
new employment areas such as space and underwater exploration and
atomic energy will add to the demand. Employment changes and
replacements for those who die, retire, or transfer to other
occupations will total well over 400,000 by 1980, an average of
almost 45,000 annually.

    A recent study conducted by the AAJC [2] under the sponsorship
of the Bureau of Health Manpower determined that the number of
graduates from allied health occupational training programs swelled
from approximately 5,000 in 1960 to over 34,000 in 1970. The
variety of training opportunities ranged from home aide to two-year
Associate of Arts degree nurse.

    One of the fastest-growing occupations, staffed primarily by
women, is the field of dental hygienics. By 1980 total employment
in this sector is expected to reach 33,500, an increase of
approximately 109 percent over the 16,000 employment figure for
1968. The demand for hygienists is expected to increase as a result of
the expanding demand for dental care and increased realization on
the part of dentists that employing dental aides is good business. The
expected increase of approximately 109 percent above the 16,000
now employed in this field represents an annual rate of growth of 9.1
percent, a considerable increase over the average 2.4 percent increase
in employment during the 1960s.

    Library technicians will continue to be in great demand during this
decade. By 1980, an increase of 77 percent above the 70,000

employed in 1968 is expected. The continuing shortage of professional librarians and an expanded number of public and school libraries are the basic factors underlying this expanded requirement. Those with formal postsecondary training will continue to replace those who obtain their qualifications on the job. Employers are expected to require an A.A. degree as more formally trained library technicians become available. Since the present output of technicians is very limited (110 per year), a greatly expanded program is needed to fill the estimated 6,500 library technician job opportunities annually.

In 1968, 285,000 full-time policemen were employed in local police departments. By 1980, employment requirements for police officers are expected to reach 360,000, an increase of 27 percent. As cities increase in size and complexity, police forces must be expanded to meet the demand. Emphasis upon advanced training in sociology, psychology, and minority group relations will heighten the demand for some postsecondary education. Annual openings, estimated at 15,000 to fill new slots and to replace those who change jobs, retire, or die, will have to be filled. Since only about 2,000 persons are graduated each year from police academies and community colleges, the number will have to be expanded rapidly to keep up with the demand, particularly for police officers who require special law enforcement training.

This sampling of occupations underscores the need for an aggressive response by community colleges to changing requirements and opportunities. Many of these occupations, because of their social service orientation, will appeal to a broad cross section of students from a variety of socioeconomic backgrounds. Service to humanity strikes a resonant chord among many in the younger generation who feel the need (and, to some extent, the peer-group pressure) to help close the gap between the promise and the reality of a democratic society. Many from more affluent backgrounds are motivated to serve those who are less fortunate. Those from disadvantaged backgrounds will continue to be motivated by extrinsic rewards, but many will want to return to their neighborhoods to help those who are less fortunate. Both groups will find ample opportunities for self-realization in the "helping" professions.

Of the estimated 4 million job openings each year during the 1970s, 40 percent will require some form of postsecondary education. Many of these, while nonprofessional in nature, represent the expanding employment opportunity of the future.

WORK AND THE NEW STUDENT

The shift in the population gravity center from late adolescence to early adulthood not only will result in an increased competition for jobs requiring more than a high school diploma, but will bring with it a reemphasis upon the traditional values of thrift, self-reliance, and achievement during this decade. The current concerns of the adolescent, e.g., achieving independence from parents, developing a personal sense of identity, and gaining social and economic status, while still important areas of emphasis, [36] will not be the paramount concerns of the junior college student, who, on the average, will be older than his four-year college contemporary. The college students of the 1960s did pretty much what they wanted to do, with some focusing their attention on dissent and protest. Such activities will give way to the desire to qualify for employment in order to meet their own and their families' needs. Stiff job competition will leave less time for other pursuits.

The interest in gainful employment will not necessarily reflect a return to those values associated with the Protestant ethic, however. Work (and its attendant benefits) will no longer be viewed as an end in and of itself. In spite of the President's plea to return to the work ethic of the past, many workers will be looking for employment opportunities which will allow them to serve mankind but, at the same time, enable them to enjoy a sense of self-fulfillment or to pursue leisure-time interests. Some will elect to invest their increased leisure time in upgrading their work skills in order to qualify for higher levels of responsibility. Others will seek to enhance their artistic skills in the interest of self-expression.

The student of the 1970s will be more tolerant of ambiguity, will be more rational in his career decisions, and will evidence greater maturity than his predecessor of the 1960s. He will be the product of a shrinking world. Through travel and television he will have witnessed the discrepancies between the values of the older generation and their behavior. His sensitivity to inequality of opportunity and to all the other unrealized promises of a democratic society will make him want to redress this inconsistency through his own efforts. His career interests will permit him to serve mankind while avoiding the trap of poverty himself.

The increased participation of older students in our community junior colleges will create a more mature and stable climate at these institutions. Who are these potential students? Our interviews with a broad cross section of students gave us some clues. A number of women that we interviewed during the span of the study reported that they were preparing for second careers now that they had successfully raised their children. For some this took the form of strengthening or updating already acquired skills. For others, it represented earning additional credits towards an A.A. or B.A. degree.

Many of the part-time male students whom we interviewed were seeking to change their occupations or to qualify for higher levels of responsibility and income. For others, this represented a chance to update their skills in their chosen field. And for still others, it meant more intellectual stimulation and rediscovery of the rewards of a "liberal education."

Returning veterans will make up an increasingly large percentage of both the full-time and part-time enrollees. Almost a third of the returning Vietnam war veterans have elected to enroll in a local community or junior ·college. As benefits like the GI Bill or comparable federal support programs become more available, it is anticipated that more and more students from all walks of life will want to take advantage of the opportunity for a college education.

SHIFTING VALUES

To attempt to trace the persisting and emergent values of our society and predict their impact on the nation's educational institutions is a chancy undertaking. The more abstract or all-pervading values such as "honesty," "justice," and "democracy" will continue to shape individual behavior in this country, but there are several emerging values which stand out from our survey data: (1) acceptance and reevaluation of the concept of equal educational opportunity, particularly as it applies to the "right" of access to at least two years of postsecondary education; (2) emergence of a consumer ethic in conjunction with what some have labeled our postindustrial society; and (3) a growing awareness of the rewards of contemplation and creative self-expression in an increasingly automated and mechanized society.

Federal support for a postsecondary education for all (with its attendant emphasis upon expanded student loans) demonstrates congressional endorsement of the concept of universal education for at least 14 years. Minority group members and students from low socioeconomic status have come to accept access to postsecondary education as a right, not a privilege. This egalitarian concept is strongly supported not only by minority group members and the disenfranchised but by those of middle-class and upper-middle-class origins. Such expectations have already reshaped the institutions of higher learning. Open colleges, external degree programs, "universities without walls," these mechanisms are designed to make college available to any and all potential enrollees. The demand for access will increase during the decade and become more and more a central issue in any federally sponsored program.

The postindustrial society has been characterized [50] as a period of rapid expansion and consolidation of private business into larger and larger organizations, with streamlined production methods utilizing machines in place of people. This shift from human to nonhuman methods of production will result in increased leisure, pressures to spread available work opportunities, and a continuing rise in the number of people employed in supplying human services.

Higher production through automation has helped to spawn the age of the computer, a necessary instrument for controlling and linking together sprawling enterprises. The demand for computers and the need to amortize their high costs by means of increased production and greater efficiency requires administrators and technicians who are able to troubleshoot balky equipment and plan ahead. Expanded automation of many phases of the industrial process and the dehumanizing of work will lead some people to seek out jobs with a more humanistic bent. As the number of workers required to maintain our high level of productivity diminishes, so will the idea that work is an end in and of itself. Mass education and its required regimentation once helped to prepare young people for work in an industrial society. [64] When there is less emphasis upon high human productivity, the values associated with a "consumer society" will begin to take precedence.

As lower-level work opportunities become scarcer, the pressure for a more equitable distribution of such opportunities and the resultant increase in leisure time will give rise to a new set of values associated with the "nonproductive" uses of such leisure. Much of our leisure time will continue to be expended in three areas: play, contemplation, and service to others. Community junior colleges will enhance the use of leisure in at least two of these three areas. Older workers, accustomed to a work ethic, will need to be assisted, through education, to shift to a "leisure ethic." Younger adults will want to develop work skills which will make it possible for them to serve others. Both groups will need to become more consumption-oriented.

IMPLICATIONS FOR COMMUNITY JUNIOR COLLEGES

These emerging social values have profound implications for the future role of community junior colleges. If, as we suggest, tomorrow's two-year college student will be the product of a shrinking world, seeking a more internally consistent set of values, then our institutions must be ready to respond to such expectations or be prepared to bear the brunt of student activism. Tomorrow's student will evidence greater concern with shaping his own destiny. Curriculum offerings and institutional procedures need to be planned with student participation. Independent study opportunities, more flexible course schedules, and greater attention to individual learning styles will be required. College students are demanding that the learning process be shaped to *their* requirements and not arranged just for the benefit of the faculty and staff.

Faculty members working with such students will be expected to be more open, honest, and democratic. An atmosphere of equality and interest in the student will emerge. College administrators will want to respond to community needs, particularly those that represent employment opportunities for graduates. Institutionally based, discipline-centered programs will give way to learner-centered, community-oriented programs. Educational opportunities will be provided where the potential student lives or works, with course offerings adjusted to his requirements on a part-time basis or in concentrated periods.

The vitality and rapid growth of community junior colleges during the last decade has helped to underscore the appeal that this form of higher education has. Increased competition for scarce dollar resources and, eventually, for more students suggests that the community-oriented college can no longer get by on promises alone. A shifting population base and the changing character of our work ethic should serve to forewarn those administrators who are futuristically oriented that their institutions must respond in appropriate ways or go under.

CHANGING CHARACTER OF THE COMMUNITY

Willingham, [70] Peterson, [55] and others have observed that one of the causes of student protest is the absence of concern among faculty members with solving the problems of the larger community. A focus on the problems of the community and the need to serve the "new" student more effectively has brought the community colleges into center stage as the potential mechanism for meeting community and individual student needs. The impression that some institutions (most frequently four-year institutions) give of being "above the fray" is hardly calculated to win the support of the community. As we saw in Chapter 3, even community college presidents and faculty tend to place concern with social issues and community problems well down on their list of priority issues, while students place the "formulation of programs in a number of public policy areas such as pollution control" among the upper half of the goals to be served by their institutions. Serving the needs of the community and developing more flexible ways of assisting the marginal student emerged from our study as among the top-ranking priorities for community colleges during this decade.

America, as a modern industrial society, has become increasingly urbanized. Lecht observes that "by 1975, over three-fourths of all Americans will be living in urban areas. . . . As urbanization proceeds, expanding metropolitan centers will emerge to form a new social and economic unit—the megalopolis." [45] Not only will the concentration of population in about five megalopolitan centers bring with it problems of transportation, recreation, housing, and land and water use, but it will also place new demands on community junior colleges. The rapid in-out migration of persons in many of our nation's population centers, coupled with the changing ethnic, socioeconomic, and age composition of these populations, makes it virtually impossible for anyone to "know" his community without making a conscientious and continuing effort to do so.

A more effective linkage of the community college with its constituents would serve two purposes: (1) it would help the college assess the expectations of the community, and (2) it would help the community to become more aware of the policies and programs of the college. The latter function is receiving increased attention, but the former function has yet to be addressed systematically. If the college is concerned with an effective two-way communication program, then it must survey community feelings and expectations and follow through with effective responses to the survey results. Other, perhaps less systematic, means for involvement of community representatives through advisory committees, the board of trustees, and periodic open forums will also be needed if community expectations are to be understood and effectively served.

The growing interest in community service programs and lifelong learning or continuing education programs has been outlined in

Chapter 5. The demand for such learning opportunities and relevant community services will continue to rise, paralleling the mix of age groups and ethnic backgrounds in the community. The use of the college facility as a lifelong learning center, as a place for convening community-oriented workshops, and as a meeting place for community organizations will continue to expand. The number of community-based advisory groups, many representing the special interests of local employers, minority groups, older age groups, etc., is also likely to grow. While the response of community colleges to these local interests has in the past been uneven, new prototype systems are now emerging which can serve as models for the future.

GOVERNANCE STRUCTURES FOR THE 1970S

Bold responses to education and training needs as outlined are in order. More rational planning and decision-making procedures must be developed, with continued attention to diverse student requirements. This emphasis on expanded services for community groups will necessitate some adjustment on the part of administrators and faculty. How to balance and accommodate the needed reorientation and the shifts in decision-making authority will be the focus of this last section of the chapter. In so doing, we will touch upon the roles of administrators, trustees, faculty, students, community groups, state legislators, and state educational administrators.

In the past, community colleges, unlike many of their four-year counterparts, have operated on the principle of a strong chief executive making decisions unilaterally. Faculty and students were not privy to the thinking behind most of the major decisions affecting their work or learning opportunities. Faculty groups could advise but were not often authorized to act on this advice without review by higher authority. In this sense, the governance structures of community colleges were more like the bureaucratic arrangements of public elementary and secondary schools than like other institutions of higher learning.

As this report and others [61] have demonstrated, faculty, students, and community groups will no longer sit passively while their destinies are shaped for them. Shared decision-making procedures are being implemented. The proper roles of state, district, and local institutions are now being hammered out, but their ultimate roles have yet to be identified.

We have devoted considerable attention to identifying the potential impact of these social and economic trends on community colleges. A recent study [63] found that the old structures are undergoing change. Tillery, through a nationwide survey, determined that 40 percent of the public community college presidents anticipate some change in their organizational structure within the next two or three years. Departmental structures are no longer the preferred pattern of organization unless they are grouped under larger divisions. He found more interest in interdisciplinary structures, reflecting a shift from the traditional subject-matter department to problem-oriented or career program-oriented divisional structures. Cluster college arrangements were a preferred mode of organization for approximately 20 percent of those responding to the Tillery survey, indicating an increasing interest in this concept. Community college presidents also indicated a desire to reduce the number of instructional units (70 percent of the colleges reported that they had less than 10 instructional units, e.g., a political science department, and those with more preferred fewer). This emphasis upon interdisciplinary coordination offers some hope of breaking down the traditional communication barriers between instructional units within the conventional college structure.

Tillery also found that presidents tended to feel that their current structures were designed to satisfy the concerns of faculty members but not designed to respond to student or community needs. Our own survey findings reflect this same attitude. A number of presidents observed that they saw structures determining goals and not, as one might expect, the other way around.

Obsolete structures which primarily benefit staff members will no longer be tolerated. The key will be to evolve a results-oriented administrative system where the success of the institution will be judged in terms of the impact it has on students and on the community. Specifying goals and objectives in terms of the output—improving student performance, resolving community problems—of the institution makes it possible to incorporate a new array of learning and administrative procedures, accepting those that work and getting rid of obsolete or nonproductive practices.

One caveat, however, needs to be stated. A results-oriented approach to administration, if applied without consideration of the interests of those directly involved, can foster resistance on the part of faculty or other staff if imposed from the top down in the name of "scientific management." Shared decision making and a sense of participation can help to alleviate this potential hazard to the community junior college (see Chapter 4).

Chief executives at the local level not only must learn to share their decision-making authority with others at this level but must be increasingly concerned with the concentration of power at the state level. Wattenbarger [69] has expressed his concern over this seemingly irreversible trend. He observes that where local control persists, community colleges enjoy rapid expansion, e.g., California, Florida, Michigan, Illinois, and New York; but where control was centralized at the state level, their growth and responsiveness to community needs has not been as great. The variety of curriculum offerings is richer where local control prevails. Wattenbarger concludes that the "locally operated junior colleges were more faithful to the philosophical criteria which are generally used to identify the community junior college." [69, p. 9]

Presidents are not unaware of their loss of decision-making authority. In our survey of the perceptions of community junior college presidents, we asked the question, "How influential is your local or district governing board as compared with state agencies in setting policies for each of the following functions at your college?" They were asked to judge, for several policy areas, the degree of local or state control five years ago, presently, and five years from now (responses could range from (1) "fully local" to (5) "fully state"). Chart 6.4 reveals that policies governing the selection of texts and instructional materials, the type of curriculum to be offered, and admissions were in the past, and will continue to be, the responsibility of local policy makers. On other issues, such as determining the amount of student fees and tuition, the establishment of district boundaries, determination of the size of operating and capital budgets, and educational facilities specifications, the responsibility for overall policy has moved in the direction of state control. These latter areas of concern all point to increasing responsibility at the state level.

At the campus level, presidents have recognized that trustees, faculty, and students should be more involved in decision making. This shift toward shared responsibilities in policy determination is principally the result of the rise in collective bargaining practices, the growth of multicampus districts, and the increasing maturity of the student body. When asked whether the board of trustees was taking a greater or lesser interest in the demands of various constituent groups, 57 percent of the presidents surveyed reported that trustees were showing more interest in faculty demands, 68 percent observed that trustees were more interested in student demands, and 48 percent reported that trustees were showing more interest in local

CHART 6.4   LOCAL AND STATE POLICY-MAKING CONTROL
(PUBLIC INSTITUTIONS ONLY)

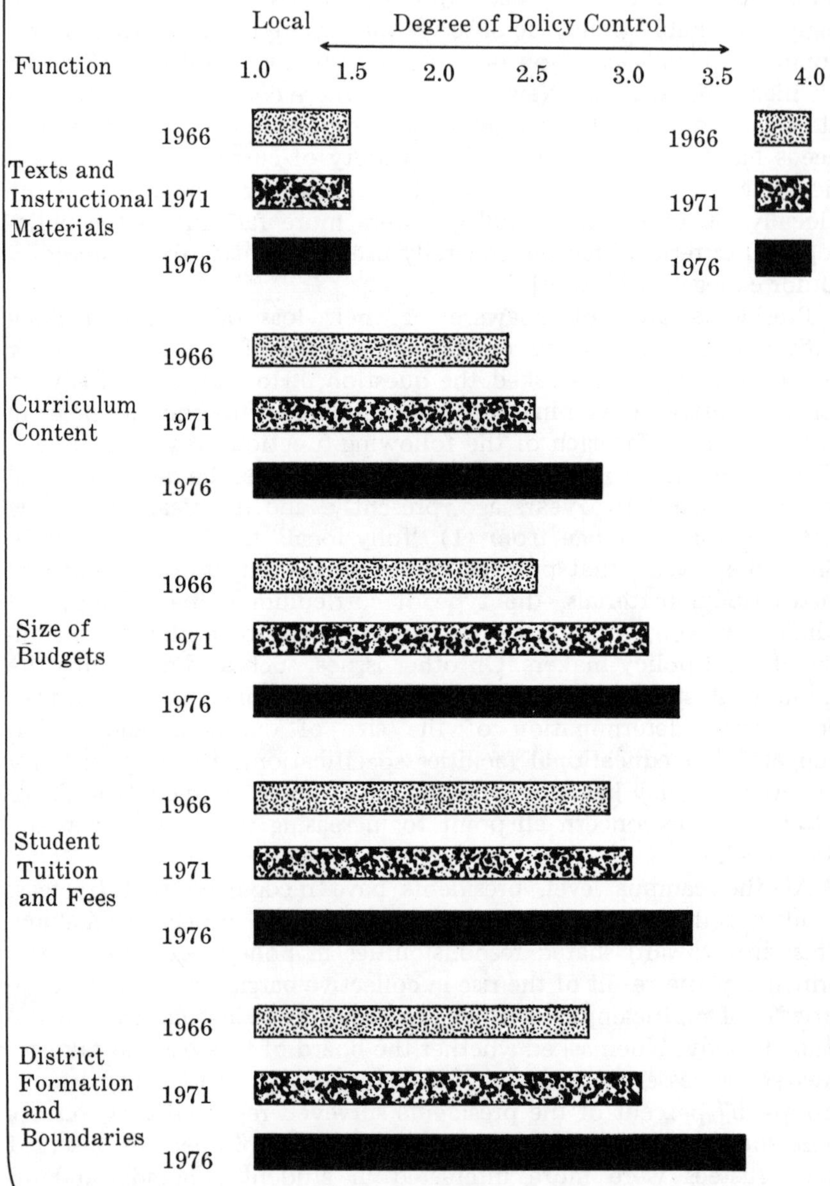

community groups. Clearly, trustees are perceived to be assuming greater responsibility and taking more interest in the needs and demands of those they represent.

While more of the decisions affecting the goals and priorities of junior colleges will be made in state capitals in the future, local institutions will be experimenting with new mechanisms for facilitating communitywide participation in decision making. The degree of influence exercised should be commensurate with the competence of the group and its potential contribution to the overall capability of the institution to achieve its goals. How and in what proportion each group is represented must reflect the extent to which it is affected by those decisions over which it will have some control. How much authority should be given to a council, a faculty senate, or an assembly, as we indicated earlier, is in the process of being hammered out.

The redistribution of authority needs to be made explicit, with each group sharing in the responsibility for implementing that authority, keeping in mind the broader interest of the institution as well as parochial interests. If students, for example, are to take responsibility for those areas which affect them more directly, e.g., dress codes, student disciplinary actions, grading practices, and instructor evaluation, then they should be held accountable for their decisions. But they must also share in the responsibility for creating an environment which facilitates learning. If faculty are to exercise responsibility for admission policies, curriculum offerings, and certification, they must be held accountable by students, administrators, and the board for the overall smooth functioning of the institution. The president will become more and more of a coordinator, required to maintain the loyalty and support of all factions making up the campus community. His principal concern will be to enunciate the goals to be served. How and who will serve them will be secondary to this overriding interest.

We foresee continued tension between state and local authorities over who will set priorities and what those priorities should be. The issue is not either/or, but really one of trying to define the appropriate role of each decision-making body to ensure that the larger public interest is met, scarce resources are allocated effectively, and those most directly affected (students, taxpayers, faculty, administrators) have an opportunity to shape those policies and decisions which affect them.

A division of labor between administrators at the campus level, at district levels, and at state levels is beginning to emerge. The task at the local level will be to implement programs which are responsive to priorities set at the district level and to identify the resources needed to carry out such programs. The district-level responsibility will be to differentiate, specify which curriculum offerings and career education opportunities are to be provided by each of the multiple institutions making up the district, and allocate funds accordingly. State agencies will be required to specify the long-range goals and priorities for districts so that statewide higher education needs are met.

With these differentiated responsibilities go the caveats: Any statewide system must permit questions of educational policy to be openly debated, and the resulting decisions must be facilitated, not inhibited, by concern for efficiency and economy. As dollar resources shrink and as the administrative tasks become more complex, it is obvious that a public community college program will require strong leadership at state, district, and local levels. Such leadership requires the ability not only to establish and implement new programs and to evaluate and modify existing ones, but also to plan and to involve those concerned in the decision-making process.

SUMMARY AND CONCLUSIONS

All evidence points to this decade as a period of consolidation and stability for community junior colleges. The movement of war babies from late adolescence to early adulthood will presage a sharp rise in the number of twenty- to thirty-five-year-olds seeking work, many for the first time. The shock of competition in the labor market will motivate these young adults to seek out entry-level occupational training as well as training for higher-level responsibilities. The demand for white-collar workers and technical-level personnel will continue to expand rapidly, particularly in the service occupations, while the number of blue-collar and production-oriented occupations will diminish. More women will be seeking to refurbish their occupational skills in order to reenter the labor market once their children reach school age.

The values associated with work will change. Rather than being perceived as the measure of a man's personal worth, work will be viewed as a means to an end. A consumer-oriented society, with its emphasis on high productivity and automation of the methods of production and the resulting need to spread the available workload, will lead to increased leisure and consumption of goods and services.

More leisure time, particularly among the middle class, will create an increasing demand for education and enrichment programs oriented toward enhancing one's avocational interests. Learning and creative self-expression will be close corollaries of the desire to utilize one's leisure in a more rewarding fashion.

The demand for equal educational opportunities will continue unabated. Disadvantaged and minority groups will continue to advocate a more equitable distribution of resources so that public education through the fourteenth grade becomes a reality for all who want to take advantage of it. The transfer of the educational cost burden from the property tax to state income and sales taxes and increased federal support will accelerate the trend towards centralization of policy making at the state level. The continued rise in the cost of education and its prominence as a budget item will force state legislators and state educational officials to scrutinize budget requests more closely and to seek alternative sources of funding. Budget pressures will bring with them a rising concern for accountability and a thorough search for greater efficiency. The competition for scarce dollars will force state education authorities to establish or revise master plans for higher education, with emphasis upon strengthening the quality of institutional leadership, faculty qualifications, responsiveness to community needs (particularly career training needs), and fund-raising capabilities. Local administrators will continue to carry the primary responsibility for assessing and meeting community needs, while state personnel will assume more and more responsibility for setting overall policies, determining the size of budgets, establishing district boundaries and facility specifications, and spelling out which long-range goals are to be served and by whom.

While enrollments in four-year institutions of higher education will even out or decline during the decade, community college enrollments will continue to climb, reaching a level of 4.5 million full- and part-time students by 1980. Students will be older, more self-directed, and more certain of their career interests.

These trends will have several effects on our nation's community junior colleges:

1 Continued support for the concept of the open door will require more effective developmental education program offerings. Tested alternatives directed at strengthening both the student's learning skills and his motivation will be needed. Faculty members will require radically improved pre- and in-service training if they are to effectively meet the needs of a diverse array of students.

2 Greatly expanded minority group enrollment will require dramatic increases in the number of minority group faculty representatives, counselors, and administrators. Expanded recruitment programs and in-service training are needed to help resolve the current imbalance between the number of minority students and faculty members.

3 Strengthened lifelong learning programs will require institutional commitments and appropriate staffing well beyond the current level. Budget procedures and administrative support mechanisms will need to be overhauled to ensure greater continuity of programming.

4 Improved ways of articulating career and transfer programs will need to be adopted if loss of credit is to be avoided by those in career-oriented programs. Clustered courses and core curricula will help to eliminate the current separation. Work-study programs, part-time enrollment, intermittent enrollment, and external degrees offer promising alternatives to traditional procedures.

5 Closer linkage of the community with the college will be achieved through systematic needs assessment and communication efforts. Off-campus course offerings, involvement of community leaders in policy making, television coverage of campus events, and outreach recruiting will help to ensure a closer collaborative relationship between the community and the college.

6 New organizational structures which encourage those who should participate in decision making to do so will emerge. The typical bureaucratic structure of the past, with its hierarchical alignment of administrators, staff, and students, will give way to a participatory management framework, with both faculty and administrators serving as "learning managers." Results-oriented goals and objectives will facilitate a more effective allocation of resources for the benefit of the student and the community.

Our country's capacity for leadership and innovation is finding one of its most noteworthy expressions in the accessibility of community junior colleges to students from diverse socioeconomic backgrounds. Demands for equal opportunity, social reforms, and self-realization can be met through these institutions. As bureaucracy and automation slowly erode our sense of individual identity, continued access to education will help us maintain and enhance our survival power in an otherwise inhospitable environment.

References

1. American Association of Junior Colleges. *1971 Junior College Directory.* Washington, D.C.: American Association of Junior Colleges, 1971.
2. American Association of Junior Colleges. *Allied Health Education Programs in Junior Colleges.* Washington, D.C.: U. S. Department of Health, Education and Welfare, Contract No. 70-4125 (in press).
3. American College Testing Program. *The Institutional Self-Study Service Manual, Part I.* Iowa City, Iowa: The American College Testing Program, Inc., 1970.
4. Baskin, Samuel. *Universities Without Walls.* Yellowsprings, Ohio: Union of Experimenting Colleges and Universities, Interim Report, 1972.
5. Batmale, Louis F., and Mullany, George H., eds. *Career Training in Hotel and Restaurant Operation at City College of San Francisco.* San Francisco, California: San Francisco City College, 1967.
6. Berls, Robert E. "Higher Education Opportunity and Achievement in the United States." *The Economics and Financing of Higher Education in the United States: A Compendium of Papers submitted to the Joint Economic Committee, Congress of the United States.* Washington, D.C.: U. S. Congress, 1969.
7. Bloom, Benjamin S. "Learning for Mastery." *U.C.L.A. Evaluation Comment,* Vol. 1, No. 2, 1968.
8. Bogue, Jesse P. *The Community College.* New York: McGraw-Hill, 1950.
9. Boocock, Sarane S. and Schild, E. O., eds. *Simulation Games in Learning.* Beverly Hills, California: Sage Publications, Inc., 1968.

10. Bureau of Labor Statistics. *College Educated Workers, 1968-80.* Washington, D.C.: U. S. Department of Labor, 1970.

11. Bureau of Labor Statistics. *The U. S. Economy in 1980.* Washington, D.C.: U. S. Department of Labor, Bulletin 1673, 1970.

12. Bushnell, David S. "A Suggested Guide for Developing a Systems Approach to Curriculum Improvements." In Heidenreich, R. R., ed., *Improvements in Curriculum.* Arlington, Virginia: College Readings Inc., 1972.

13. Bushnell, David S., and Rappaport, Donald. *Planned Change in Education.* New York: Harcourt Brace Jovanovich, 1971.

14. Carnegie Commission on Higher Education. *The Capital and the Campus: State Responsibility for Postsecondary Education.* New York: McGraw-Hill, 1971.

15. Carnegie Commission on Higher Education. *Less Time, More Options: Education Beyond the High School.* New York: McGraw-Hill, 1971.

16. Carnegie Commission on Higher Education. *New Students and New Places.* New York: McGraw-Hill, 1971.

17. Carnegie Commission on Higher Education. *The Open Door Colleges: Policies for Community Colleges.* New York: McGraw-Hill, 1970.

18. *Chronicle of Higher Education,* Vol. 6, No. 12, December 13, 1971.

19. Cogan, Eugene A. "Systems Analysis and the Introduction of Educational Technology in Schools." In Sidney G. Tickton, ed., *To Improve Learning, An Evaluation of Instructional Technology, Part Two, Selected Working Papers on the State of the Art.* New York: R. R. Bowker Company, Vol. II, 1970.

20. Cohen, Arthur M. *Dateline '79: Heretical Concepts for the Community College.* Beverly Hills, California: Glencoe Press, 1969.

21. Compensatory Education Project. *Reaching for the Ideal: A Set of Recommendations to Texas Community Junior Colleges.* Austin, Texas: Junior College Division, Coordinating Board, Texas College and University System, 1971.

22. *Computerized Vocational Information System.* Glen Ellyn, Illinois: College of DuPage, 1971.

23. Cross, K. Patricia. "Occupationally Oriented Students." *Junior College Research Review,* Vol. 5, No. 3, November 1970.

24. Dawson, Dudley J. *The Masters College Program.* Yellowsprings, Ohio: Union for Experimenting Colleges and Universities, March 1971.

25. Drucker, Peter. "The Surprising Seventies." *Harper's Magazine,* Vol. 243: 35-9, September 1971.

26. Educational Policies Commission. *Universal Opportunity for Education Beyond High School.* Washington, D.C.: National Education Association, 1964.

27. Empire State College. *Interim Report: 1971-72.* Saratoga Springs, New York: Empire State College—SUNY, 1972.

28. Flanagan, John. "How Instructional Systems Will Manage Learning." *Nation's Schools,* Vol. 86, No. 4, October 1970.

29. Garrison, Roger H. *Junior College Faculty: Issues and Problems. A Preliminary National Appraisal.* Washington, D.C.: American Association of Junior Colleges, 1967.

30. Godfrey, Eleanor P., and Holmstrom, Engin I. *Study of Community Colleges and Vocational-Technical Centers, Phase I.* Washington, D.C.: Bureau of Social Science Research, 1970.

31. Gross, Edward. "Universities as Organizations: A Research Approach." *American Sociological Review,* August 1968.

32. Gross, Edward and Grambsch, Paul. *University Goals and Academic Power.* Washington, D.C.: American Council on Education, 1968.

33. Hanson, Lee and Weisbroad, Burton A. "The Distribution of Direct Costs and Benefits of Public Higher Education." *Journal of Human Resources,* Spring 1969.

34. Harris, Norman C. "Curriculum and Instruction in Occupational Education." *Emphasis: Occupational Education in the Two-Year College.* Washington, D.C.: American Association of Junior Colleges, 1966.

35. Havelock, Ronald. *A Guide to Innovation in Education.* Ann Arbor, Michigan: Center for Research on the Utilization of Scientific Knowledge, University of Michigan, 1970.

36. Havighurst, Robert J. *Human Development and Education.* New York: David McKay, Inc., 1953.

37. Hendrix, Vernon L. *Functional Relationships of Junior College Environments and Selected Characteristics of Faculties, Students, the Administration, and the Community.* Washington, D.C.: U. S. Department of Health, Education and Welfare, Office of Education, Project No. 5-0770, June 1967.

38. Hitt, William D. *A Model for Humanistic Management.* Columbus, Ohio: Battelle Center for Improved Education, 1972.

39. Hutchins, Robert M. Reported in Burt Schwartz, "Is it Really Higher Education?" *Saturday Review.* New York: Saturday Review, Inc., December 19, 1964.

40. Jencks, Christopher, and Reisman, David. *The Academic Revolution.* Garden City, New York: Doubleday, 1968.

41. Katz, Martin. "Can Computers Make Guidance Decisions for Students?" *College Board Review.* Vol. 72, Summer 1969.

42. Koos, Leonard. *The Junior College.* Minneapolis, Minnesota: University of Minnesota Press, Education Series No. 5, 1924.

43. Krumboltz, John, et al. *Vocational Problem Solving Experiment for Simulating Career Exploration and Interest.* Washington, D.C.: U. S. Office of Education, Final Report, No. 5-0072, 1967.

44. *The Lange Book: Collected Writings of a Great Educational Philosopher.* A. H. Chamberlain, ed. San Francisco, California: Tray Publishing, 1927.

45. Lecht, Leonard. *Goals Priorities and Dollars.* New York: The Free Press, 1966.

46. Losak, John, *et al. Psychological Characteristics of the Academically Underprepared Student.* Miami, Florida: Miami-Dade Junior College, North Campus, 1969.

47. Matson, Jane. "A Perspective on Student Personnel Services." *Junior College Journal,* Vol. 42, No. 6, March 1972.

48. Medsker, Leland L. *The Junior College: Progress and Prospect.* New York: McGraw-Hill, 1960.

49. Medsker, Leland L., and Tillery, Dale. *Breaking the Access Barriers: A Profile of Two-Year Colleges.* New York: McGraw-Hill, 1971.

50. Michael, Donald. *The Next Generation: The Prospects Ahead for the Youth of Today and Tomorrow.* New York: Vintage Books, 1965.

51. Moses, Stanley. "Notes on the Future of Education." *Policy Research Center Report.* Syracuse, New York: Syracuse University, Vol. 1, Issue 2, January, 1970.

52. Newman, Frank, et al. *Report on Higher Education.* Washington, D.C.: U. S. Department of Health, Education and Welfare, 1971.

53. Nunney, Derek and Hill, Joseph E. "Personalized Education Programs." *Audiovisual Instruction,* February 1972.

54. Park, Young. *Junior College Faculty: Their Values and Perceptions.* Washington, D.C.: American Association of Junior Colleges, ERIC Monograph Series, Monograph 12, 1970.

55. Peterson, Richard E. *The Scope of Organized Student Protest in 1967-68.* Princeton, New Jersey: Educational Testing Service, 1968. See also Gaddy, Dale. *The Scope of Organized Student Protest in Junior Colleges.* Washington, D.C.: American Association of Junior Colleges, 1970.

56. President's Commission on Higher Education. *Higher Education for American Democracy.* New York: Harper and Brothers, Volume 1, 1947.

57. Raines, Max R. "The Student Personnel Situation." *Junior College Journal,* Vol. 36, February 1966.

58. Raines, Max, and Myran, Gunder. "Community Services: Goals for 1980." *Junior College Journal,* Vol. 42, No. 1, April 1972.

59. Roueche, John. *Salvage, Redirection, or Custody? Remedial Education in the Community Junior College.* Washington, D.C.: American Association of Junior Colleges, ERIC Monograph Series, Monograph 1, 1968.

60. Somers, Gerald G. and Fernbach, Susan B. *An Analysis of the Economic Benefits of Vocational Education at the Secondary, Postsecondary, and Junior College Levels: A Preliminary Report on an Evaluation of the Effectiveness of Vocational and Technical Education in the United States.* Madison, Wisconsin: University of Wisconsin, Center for Studies in Vocational and Technical Education, 1970. See also Davison, Mildred. *Career Graduates: A Profile of Job Experience and Further Study of Students with AAS Degrees.* New York: City University of New York, Office of Community College Affairs, August 1971.

61. Spiegel, Hans B. C. "College Relating to Community: Service To Symbiosis." *Junior College Journal,* Vol. 41, No. 1, August-September 1970.

62. Striner, Herbert E. *Continuing Education as a National Capital Investment.* Kalamazoo, Michigan: The W. E. Upjohn Institute for Employment Research, 1971.

63. Tillery, Dale. *Variation and Change in Community College Organization: A Preliminary Report.* Berkeley, California: Center for Research and Development in Higher Education, 1970.

64. Toffler, Alvin. *Future Shock.* New York: Random House, Inc. 1970.

65. Uhl, Norman. "A Technique for Improving Communication within an Institution." *Communication of Institutional Research: Proceedings of the 10th Annual Forum.* Aburn, Alabama: Aburn University, Association for Institutional Research, 1970.

66. U.S. Bureau of the Census. *Undergraduate Enrollment in Two-Year and Four-Year Colleges: October 1970.* Washington, D.C.: Current Population Reports, Series P-20, No. 231, February 1972.

67. U.S. Bureau of the Census. Unpublished data from the 1970 Census.

68. Valley, John R. *A Supplement to an Inventory of External Degree Programs and Proposals.* Princeton, New Jersey: Educational Testing Service, May 1971.

69. Wattenbarger, James. "Changing Patterns of Control: Local to State." *Junior College Journal,* Vol. 38, No. 8, May 1968.

70. Willingham, Warren W. *Free Access to Higher Education.* New York: College Entrance Examination Board, 1970.

71. Winston, Chester. "The Self Perceived and Self Reported Scope, Quality, and Staffing Patterns of Community Service Programs in 100 Community Colleges in the United States." Unpublished doctoral dissertation, Michigan State University, Lansing, Michigan, 1971.

Appendix A.
Methodology

To obtain the information necessary to achieve the objectives of Project Focus, a literature search and communication links with existing data banks on community junior colleges were established. Structured interviews, site visits, and survey questionnaires (administered to community junior college presidents, campus coordinators, students, and faculty) were utilized to obtain relevant data from a nationwide sample of community junior colleges. Various resource and advisory groups were convened for their reaction to and interpretation of findings.

This appendix provides a description of the sampling plan and other data collection procedures used in the study.

PROJECT FOCUS SAMPLE SELECTION PROCEDURE

A two-stage sampling design was used: the first stage provided a stratified sample of community and junior colleges, and the second a random selection of respondents within the selected institutions. Various kinds of weights (explained on page 150) were required to make appropriate estimates of population parameters from the data obtained in the survey samples.

Universe of Community Junior Colleges

The first step in selecting the sample of colleges to be utilized in this study was to determine the universe of community junior colleges. Realizing that the number of institutions included in a community junior college universe depends on the definition employed,[1] the community junior college listing in the *1970 Junior College Directory*, published by the American Association of Community and Junior Colleges, was adopted. For logistic reasons, only colleges in the continental United States were considered—excluding colleges from Alaska, Hawaii, Puerto Rico, etc. Although AACJC includes within its count two-year branch campuses of four-year institutions, those two-year campuses which, in the opinion of the research staff, did not function as community junior colleges and in reality were integral parts of their respective parent institutions were also excluded from the universe. Thus, 56 two-year campuses from the states of Ohio, Pennsylvania, South Carolina, and Wisconsin were eliminated. After adopting these two qualifications, 956 community junior colleges remained in the universe to be sampled: 721 public, 107 independent (nonprofit), and 128 church-related institutions.

Sample Stratification

The universe of community junior colleges was then stratified according to geographic area, size, and type: public, church-related, or independent. The following illustration depicts the manner of stratification (see Figure A-1).

The universe was separated according to public, church-related, or independent. The latter two were not broken down any further. The public colleges were classified into six geographic regions (see Table A-1). The six regions are identical with the ones used by Vernon Hendrix in his earlier study of the impact of the two-year college environment on students. [34]

In general, the regions were selected so that (1) no single state dominated a region in number of colleges (for this reason, California was made a separate region); (2) the colleges were fairly evenly distributed among the regions (see Table A-2); and (3) the regions encompassed geographically, economically, and culturally similar areas, i.e., the regions were similar to those generally used by economists, sociologists, etc. (See, for example, the analysis conducted by J. M. Richards, Jr., L. P. Rand, and L. M. Rand[2] on the regional differences in community junior colleges.)

---

[1] The number of community junior colleges reported by the American Association of Community and Junior Colleges has traditionally been larger than that reported by the U.S. Office of Education. This is the result of different criteria. The AACJC criteria for inclusion are somewhat more flexible than those of the U.S.O.E. For example, two-year branch campuses are included. Not all institutions listed in the *Directory* are members of the AACJC.

[2] J. M. Richards, Jr., L. P. Rand, and L. M. Rand, "Regional Differences in Junior Colleges," *The Two-Year College and Its Students: An Empirical Report* (American College Testing Program, Inc., Iowa City, Iowa, November 1969) pp. 27–40.

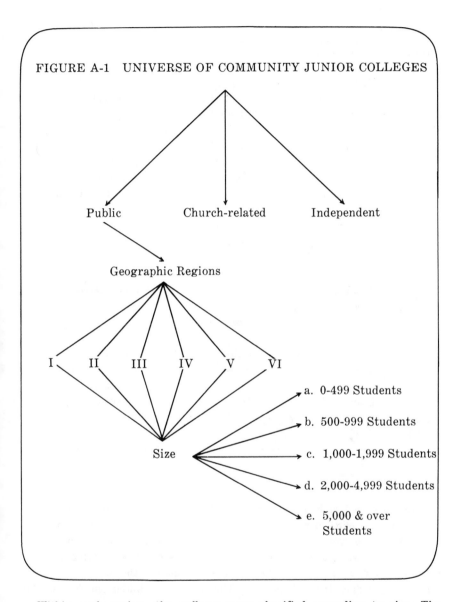

FIGURE A-1   UNIVERSE OF COMMUNITY JUNIOR COLLEGES

Within each region, the colleges were classified according to size. The completed stratification resulted in 32 cells to be used for sampling purposes (see Table A-3).

Sample Selection of Institutions

The actual sample of colleges used was arrived at through a series of steps. An initial 10 percent sample of each cell was decided upon. The colleges within each

TABLE A-1

Region	States		
I	Maine	Massachusetts	Pennsylvania
	New Hampshire	Connecticut	New Jersey
	Vermont	Rhode Island	New York
II	Delaware	North Carolina	Alabama
	Maryland	South Carolina	Kentucky
	Virginia	Georgia	Tennessee
	West Virginia	Florida	District of Columbia
III	Minnesota	Wisconsin	Ohio
	Iowa	Illinois	
	Michigan	Indiana	
IV	Washington	Idaho	South Dakota
	Oregon	Wyoming	Nebraska
	Montana	North Dakota	
V	Arizona	Colorado	Missouri
	New Mexico	Kansas	Arkansas
	Nevada	Texas	Louisiana
	Utah	Oklahoma	Mississippi
VI	California		

cell were arranged alphabetically and numbered accordingly, from "1" to the number in the particular cell. Utilizing a random table, the sample colleges within each cell were randomly picked as their number appeared until a 10 percent ceiling was reached for the cell. No cell was left at zero; each cell had to have at least one entry. Consequently, due to rounding, the overall percentage was slightly higher than 10 percent. The size of this initial sample was 100 institutions.

A letter with an accompanying post card was mailed to the presidents of the 100 institutions during the latter part of January requesting their institutions' participation in Project Focus. Twenty-one of these institutions replied in the negative. As soon as a turndown was received, the institution in question was replaced, however, with another chosen randomly from the same cell.

TABLE A-2 Number of public community junior colleges by region, enrollment, and size (in thousands)

Size Category	Region I		Region II		Region III		Region IV		Region V		Region VI		United States	
	No. of Inst.	Tot. Enr.	No. of Inst.	Tot. Enr.	No. of Inst.	Tot. Enr.	No. of Inst.	Tot. Enr.	No. of Inst.	Tot. Enr.	No. of Inst.	Tot. Enr.	No. of Inst.	Tot. Enr.
0–499	5	1.7	43	13.3	22	7.5	10	4.3	26	10.0	2	0.8	108	37.6
500–999	11	8.8	47	35.2	36	26.8	8	5.7	47	35.4	2	1.4	151	113.3
1,000–1,999	35	52.3	51	67.4	22	32.2	17	24.7	45	65.0	11	15.3	181	256.9
2,000–4,999	35	113.4	21	64.1	45	140.2	20	64.2	25	76.5	24	88.0	170	546.4
5,000 and over	14	111.9	12	105.3	18	133.2	6	53.6	9	67.6	52	552.3	111	1023.9
Total	100	288.1	174	285.3	143	339.9	61	152.5	152	254.5	91	657.8	721	1978.1

TABLE A-3   Number of public and private community junior colleges in desired
(D) and actual (A) sample, by region and size

Size	Region I D	Region I A	Region II D	Region II A	Region III D	Region III A	Region IV D	Region IV A	Region V D	Region V A	Region VI D	Region VI A	United States D	United States A
Public Colleges														
0-499	1	0	4	3	2	2	1	1	3	3	1	1	12	10
500-999	1	1	5	5	4	4	1	1	5	5	1	0	17	16
1,000-1,999	4	4	5	4	2	2	2	2	4	4	1	1	18	17
2,000-4,999	4	4	2	2	5	4	2	1	3	3	2	2	18	16
5,000 and over	1	0	1	1	2	2	1	1	2	2	5	5	12	11
Total	11	9	17	15	15	14	7	6	17	17	10	9	77	70
Private Colleges														
Church-related													13	13
Independent													10	9
Total													100	92

Due to the rather severe time limitations of Project Focus, the deadline for
obtaining replacements was set at March 26, 1971. By this date, 92 institutions
had agreed to participate. This constituted the final sample.

The institutions declining to participate were a heterogeneous group. Among
the various reasons given for refusal to participate were the following:

Our staff is hard pressed . . . We are deluged with questionnairies—more than we
can handle . . . We have a good number of time-consuming projects currently
under way and feel that time will not permit the acceptance of this worthy
project . . . We are preparing for an accreditation committee visit . . . We are
convinced that the goodwill of the faculty in responding to our requests for
assistance is essential and we hesitate to impose any burdens that might damage
this goodwill . . . The faculty and the students are becoming very sensitive about
the confidentiality of questionnaires. . . .

Table A-4 demonstrates that the turndowns are well distributed geographically. No one geographic region dominates. As indicated, all replacements were selected from the cells on a random basis. Three institutions failed to advise us before the cutoff date of March 26, 1971, of their inability to participate and therefore were not replaced.

Student Sample Selection

Each president who agreed to participate in Project Focus was asked to appoint a member of his staff to coordinate the Project Focus activities within his institution. The campus coordinators were informed, first verbally and then in writing, as to the procedures for sample selection and administering the questionnaires. One of the tasks of the campus coordinator was to select a student sample and then to administer the student questionnaire to this sample.

Campus coordinators were instructed to use the following formula for determining the number of students to be chosen for participation in the study:

If you have less than 1,000 full-time students, survey 100 (if less than 100 students, survey all).

If you have more than 1,000 but less than 10,000 full-time students, survey 10 percent.

If you have 10,000 or more full-time students, survey 5 percent.

Although the stratification of the institutions was based upon full- and part-time enrollment, the number of students chosen for the sample was to be based on the number of full-time students (not the full-time–equivalent figure commonly used at community junior colleges) enrolled during the term in which the assessment was to occur. Each college was allowed to define "full-time student" in its own way.

Although several procedures were outlined for sampling the students, the only prerequisite was that the students be randomly chosen. It was also

TABLE A-4 Distribution of turndowns by region and institutional status

	Regions						Church-related	Independent	Total
	I	II	III	IV	V	VI			
Number of refusals	2	3	3	3	2	2	3	3	21
Number in sample	9	15	14	6	17	9	13	9	92

recommended to the campus coordinators that the ratio of freshmen to sophomores at their respective institutions be reflected in their samples.

The coordinators were permitted to administer the questionnaires in any one of three ways: (1) using the class time of randomly chosen classes or classes that were required of all students, (2) bringing together the students in special scheduled group sessions, or (3) distributing the questionnaires by mail. Option #1 proved to be the most popular.

Faculty Sample Selection

The campus coordinators were also responsible for selecting the faculty sample. The faculty sample was selected according to the following formula:

If you have less than 500 full-time faculty members, survey 50 (if less than 50 faculty, survey all).

If you have more than 500 full-time faculty members, survey 10 percent.

The number of faculty members was to be based on the number of full-time, certified faculty members plus academic administrators who teach, such as deans and department chairmen. A college was allowed to use its own definition of a "full-time faculty member." Names were selected from alphabetical listings in the proportion desired. The questionnaires were to be distributed to the faculty by campus mail and returned to the coordinator in sealed envelopes.

WEIGHTING PROCEDURE

When performing sample surveys, weights are often required in order to make appropriate estimates of population parameters from the data obtained in the survey sample. Due to the rapidly changing composition of the population and the slightly less than 100 percent response rate to the questionnaires, the application of weights became a necessity. The weighting scheme utilized was developed in the Cooperative Institutional Research Program of the American Council on Education.[3]

Four types of weights, enumerated in Creager's paper, were utilized. These weights can best be illustrated by the following hypothetical example. First, let us assume that the following ground rules apply:

1 The population is divided into two strata only, with one stratum consisting of four institutions and the other of six institutions.

[3] Astin, A. W., Panos, R. J., and Creager, J. A., "A Program of Longitudinal Research on the Higher Educational System," *ACE Research Reports*, 1966, 1(1). See also John A. Creager, "Fortran Programs Providing Weights in Survey Designs Using Stratified Samples," *Educational and Psychological Measurement*, 1969, pp. 29, 709–712.

2 Only two institutions will be sampled in each stratum.

3 The number of faculty at each institution is given in the following table:

Stratum 1		Stratum 2		
a:25	b:50	e:50	f:100	g:100
c:100	d:125	h:100	i:25	j:45

The four underlined institutions (a, b, f, and h) are the ones sampled.

4 The institutions are referred to as the primary sampling units (p.s.u.'s) and the faculty members as the secondary sampling units (s.s.u.'s)

5 The participation rates or ratios in the four selected s.s.u.'s are—a: 20/25, b: 30/50, f: 65/100, and h: 85/100.

The weights utilized throughout the study were arrived at in the following way:

Type I Weights

Type I weights are used to ensure that each stratum of the population is adequately represented by the sample. Type I, or institutional cell, weights are computed for each cell as the ratio of the sum of within-institution data units across the population institutions in that cell to the sum of the within-institution data across the sample institutions in that cell. In case of the hypothetical example, the within-institution data units are the faculty members. Thus, the ratio of the population data units to the within-institution data units for the two strata, or cells, are

$$\text{Stratum 1: } 300/75 = 4.0$$
$$\text{Stratum 2: } 420/200 = 2.1$$

These weights, of course, are identical for all sampled institutions in a given stratification cell. Thus type I weights are designed to correct for inadequate cell or stratum representation.

Type II Weights

The type I weights above are sufficient if the participation rates are 100 percent. If they are not 100 percent (say, for instance, not all the faculty respond to the questionnaires), type II weights are needed. They are similar to type I weights, with the exception that individual institutions are considered rather than entire cells. Type II weights are simply the total number of s.s.u.'s per institution divided by the number of s.s.u.'s in that institution that were included in the sample. In the case of the hypothetical example, the type II weights are

a: 25/20
b: 50/30
f: 100/65
h: 100/85

Note that these weights are merely the inverses of the s.s.u. sampling fractions.

Whereas type I weights adjusted for inadequate cell or stratum representation, type II weights correct for random deviation from 100 percent participation of data units within an institution.

Type III Weights

The third type of weights are merely the product of type I and II weights. Thus, a: 4.0(1.25), b: 4.0(1.67), f: 2.1(1.54), and h: 2.1(1.18). These weights are normally applied to subsequent processing of data records developed from the within-institution sampling units.

Type IV Weights

These are institutional weights appropriate for subsequent processing of institutional unit or summary data. Type IV weights differ from type III in that the resulting estimator is in terms of p.s.u.'s instead of s.s.u.'s. They are computed for each cell and stratum as the ratio of the number of population institutions to the number of sample institutions in that cell. For example:

Stratum 1: 4/2 = 2
Stratum 2: 6/2 = 3

Theoretical Justification of the Above Weights

The estimators of the population mean and total when stratified sampling is employed are as follows:

$$\text{population mean: } \overline{y}_{st} = \sum_{h=1}^{L} \frac{N_h \overline{y}_h}{N} = \frac{\hat{Y}_{st}}{N}$$

$$\text{and total: } \hat{Y}_{st} = \sum_{h=1}^{L} N_h \overline{Y}_h$$

where $h = 1, 2, \ldots, L$ = the number of strata

N_h = the size of the hth stratum

$\overline{Y}_h$ = the sample mean of the hth stratum

$$N = \sum_{h=1}^{L} N_h = \text{the total population size}$$

Note that $\hat{Y}_{st}$ may be expressed as follows:

$$Y_{st} = \sum_{h=1}^{L} N_h \overline{y}_h$$

$$= \sum_{h=1}^{L} N_h \sum_{i=1}^{n_h} \frac{y_{hi}}{n_h}$$

(n_h is the sample size in the hth stratum)

$$= \sum_{h=1}^{L} \frac{N_h}{n_h} \sum_{i=1}^{n_h} y_{hi}$$

$$= \sum_{h=1}^{L} W_h \sum_{i=1}^{n_h} y_{hi} = \sum_{h=1}^{L} W_h y_h$$

where the W_hs are the general expressions for the weights developed above.

To illustrate the use of these formulas, consider first the situation of interest only in the p.s.u.'s. This is the situation represented by weights of type IV. In this case, as illustrated above,

$$N_1 = 4 \qquad N_2 = 6$$

$$n_1 = 2 \qquad n_2 = 2$$

Thus
$$Y_{st} = 2y_1 + 3y_2$$

Now assume that we want the variables to be expressed in terms of the faculty members, s.s.u.'s. If the participation rates at the selected institution were 100 percent,

$$\hat{Y}_{st} = 4.0y_1 + 2.1y_2 \tag{1}$$

If the participation rates were less than 100 percent, we would be forced to utilize type III weights. Then, for example,

$$\hat{Y}_{st} = 4.0\ (25/20\ y_{11} + 50/30\ y_{12}) + 2.1\ (100/65\ y_{21} + 100/85\ y_{22})\quad (2)$$

In the above formula,

   y_{11} = the total of the sampled elements in the first selected institution of the first stratum

Similarly,

   y_{12} = second institution, first stratum

   y_{21} = first institution, second stratum

   y_{22} = second institution, second stratum

Note that these type III weights reduce to type I weights if participation is complete. That is, equations (1) and (2) are then identical.

Variance of Stratified Estimators

The general expression for the estimated variance of Y_{st} is

$$\sum_{h=1}^{L} N_h^{2}\,\frac{s_h^{2}}{n_h}\left(1 - \frac{n_h}{N_h}\right)$$

where

$$s_h^{2} = \sum_{i=1}^{n_h} \frac{(y_{hi} - \bar{y}_h)^2}{n_h - 1}$$

$$= \frac{\displaystyle\sum_{i=1}^{n_h} y_{hi}^{2} - \frac{\left(\displaystyle\sum_{i=1}^{n_h} y_{hi}^{2}\right)}{n_h}}{n_h - 1}$$

DATA COLLECTION PROCEDURES

Four types of survey instruments were utilized: (1) community junior college presidents' questionnaires; (2) institutional or coordinators' questionnaires; (3) student questionnaires; (4) faculty questionnaires. See Exhibits I, II, III, and IV for examples of each questionnaire.

These survey instruments were mailed to the sample institutions by the American College Testing Program in Iowa City shortly after March 26, 1971.[4] The presidents' questionnaires were sent directly to the presidents. The other survey instruments were all sent to the campus coordinators for distribution to the respective parties, i.e., themselves, the student sample, and the faculty sample. The campus coordinators were given the responsibility for administering and returning the student, faculty, and coordinator questionnaires. After the initial surge of responses by many institutions in the sample, telephone calls were made to the nonresponding campus coordinators and college presidents urging them to complete and return their questionnaires as soon as possible. A second mailing to nonresponding presidents was made in April 1971. July 30, 1971, was established as a final cutoff date for mailing in all questionnaires.

RESPONSE RATES

The response rate to the presidents' questionnaires was near perfect—98 percent. Ninety of the 92 presidents who had agreed to participate in Project Focus completed their questionnaires. The response rate to the institutional questionnaire, filled out by the campus coordinator, was 75 percent—a respectably sized sample in its own right. Fifty-one of the 70 public two-year college coordinators responded. In both cases, several telephone calls were made to the respective parties, encouraging them to complete their questionnaires. While no systematic study of nonresponding coordinators was conducted, explanations provided by telephone can largely be summarized as either the data was unavailable or those having the needed information were unwilling to cooperate. In a few cases, the person assigned by the president to the task felt unqualified to complete it.

Student and faculty responses were aggregated at the institutional level. The response rate and resultant weights were determined as the ratio of complete respondents to the sample chosen at each institution. Table A-5 presents the detailed breakdown. For each institution the following information is given: (1) size of student sample chosen, (2) number of student respondents, (3) percent of student response [ratio of (1) to (2)], (4) size of faculty sample chosen, (5) number of faculty respondents, and (6) percent of faculty response.

We arbitrarily decided in advance to include in the study only those sets of students or faculty whose response rate was higher than 75 percent. However, this criterion was modified to include a number of institutions, mainly larger ones, which otherwise would have been eliminated from the analysis or were needed for adequate representation in each cell. In these instances, the response

---

[4] Throughout the study, ACT provided assistance in questionnaire design and development, survey instrument distribution and collection, and data computerization and analysis.

TABLE A-5   Student and faculty response

Institution	Stud. Samp. Chosen	Student Respondents	Student Resp. Rate	Fac. Samp. Chosen	Faculty Respondents	Fac. Resp. Rate
#1.	110	110	100.0%	21	16	76.2%
2.	145	131	90.3	49	48	98.0
3.	150	124	82.7	54	42	77.8
4.	179	176	98.3	40	40	100.0
5.	120	91	75.8	—	—	—
6.	100	100	100.0	37	35	94.6
7.	129	126	97.7	60	59	98.3
8.	100	97	97.0	55	51	92.7
9.	800	659	82.4	40	37	92.5
10.	111	107	96.4	47	42	89.4
11.	161	161	100.0	59	57	96.6
12.	300	232	77.3	60	54	90.0
13.	103	101	98.1	30	30	100.0
14.	100	100	100.0	41	39	95.1
15.	110	96	87.3	56	51	91.1
16.	115	108	93.9	33	31	93.9
17.	100	88	88.0	30	30	100.0
18.	146	90	61.6*	50	48	96.0
19.	116	116	100.0	34	32	94.1
20.	107	78	72.9*	—	—	—
21.	128	102	79.7	50	43	86.0
22.	204	105	51.5*	49	41	83.7
23.	130	102	78.5	10	8	80.0
24.	107	107	100.0	47	40	85.1
25.	100	83	83.0	—	—	—
26.	129	118	91.5	64	64	100.0
27.	200	196	98.0	49	39	79.6
28.	154	154	100.0	49	49	100.0
29.	101	101	100.0	40	40	100.0
30.	125	85	68.0*	60	56	93.3
31.	100	80	80.0	—	—	—
32.	113	100	88.5	14	14	100.0
33.	160	145	90.6	—	—	—
34.	102	96	94.1	47	47	100.0
35.	162	104	64.2*	—	—	—
36.	142	127	89.4	47	44	93.6
37.	66	66	100.0	5	4	80.0
38.	163	161	98.8	63	48	76.2
39.	90	76	84.4	11	8	72.7*
40.	108	108	100.0	19	18	94.7
41.	102	102	100.0	28	24	85.7
42.	100	95	95.0	—	—	—
43.	100	98	98.0	50	48	96.0

TABLE A-5 (Continued)

Institution	Stud. Samp. Chosen	Student Respondents	Student Resp. Rate	Fac. Samp. Chosen	Faculty Respondents	Fac. Resp. Rate
44.	100	95	95.0%	49	49	100.0%
45.	110	102	92.7	32	30	93.8
46.	140	88	62.9*	49	47	95.9
47.	100	76	76.0	39	32	82.1
48.	142	142	100.0	—	—	—
49.	452	400	88.5	44	34	77.3
50.	122	101	82.8	12	12	100.0
51.	100	100	100.0	26	26	100.0
52.	100	78	78.0	30	23	76.7
53.	120	103	85.8	24	23	95.8
54.	107	106	99.1	24	24	100.0
55.	124	122	98.4	49	47	95.9
56.	103	103	100.0	33	33	100.0
57.	128	128	100.0	—	—	—
58.	100	82	82.0	53	53	100.0
59.	143	137	95.8	48	36	75.0
60.	55	55	100.0	—	—	—
61.	191	162	84.8	50	47	94.0
62.	448	271	60.5*	53	51	96.2
63.	100	100	100.0	29	29	100.0
64.	103	94	91.3	49	37	75.5
65.	100	98	98.0	50	42	84.0
66.	560	512	91.4	58	50	86.2
67.	1125	754	67.0*	44	44	100.0
68.	266	258	97.0	—	—	—
69.	130	112	86.2	16	16	100.0
70.	98	96	98.0	26	26	100.0
71.	355	301	84.8	59	49	83.1
72.	112	112	100.0	13	11	84.6
73.	- - -	- - -	- - -	—	—	—
74.	- - -	- - -	- - -	11	11	100.0
75.	- - -	- - -	- - -	40	39	97.5
76.	- - -	- - -	- - -	66	56	84.8
77.	- - -	- - -	- - -	40	33	82.5
78.	- - -	- - -	- - -	48	40	83.3
79.	- - -	- - -	- - -	49	43	87.8
80.	- - -	- - -	- - -	—	—	—
81.	- - -	- - -	- - -	—	—	—
82.	- - -	- - -	- - -	30	21	70.0*
83.	- - -	- - -	- - -	- - -	- - -	- - -
84.	- - -	- - -	- - -	- - -	- - -	- - -
85.	- - -	- - -	- - -	- - -	- - -	- - -
86.	- - -	- - -	- - -	- - -	- - -	- - -

TABLE A-5 (Continued)

Institution	Stud. Samp. Chosen	Student Respondents	Student Resp. Rate	Fac. Samp. Chosen	Faculty Respondents	Fac. Resp. Rate
87.	- - -	- - -	- - -	- - -	- - -	- - -
88.	- - -	- - -	- - -	- - -	- - -	- - -
89.	- - -	- - -	- - -	- - -	- - -	- - -
90.	- - -	- - -	- - -	- - -	- - -	- - -
91.	- - -	- - -	- - -	- - -	- - -	- - -
92.	- - -	- - -	- - -	- - -	- - -	- - -

Ledger:
—   Excluded from study due to insufficient response (less than 75 percent).
- - -   Excluded from study due to no returns at all.
*   Institutions, mainly large ones, included in the study with less than 75 percent
       response rate to allow adequate representation in each cell.

rate could be no lower than 50 percent. These institutions are identified by an asterisk.

A special questionnaire was sent to the campus coordinators after they had administered the student and faculty questionnaires to determine the size of the student and faculty samples which they had chosen. In cases of no response to this questionnaire, a telephone call was made and the needed information obtained. This questionnaire also incorporated questions on sampling procedure and how they went about administering the questionnaire.

Of those institutions included in the final analysis, the total number of students sampled is 12,022; the total number of usable student respondents is 10,250, yielding a response rate of 85.6 percent. The total number of faculty sampled is 2,741; the total amount of usable faculty respondents is 2,491, yielding a response rate of 90.9. Due to the acceptable response rate by both students and faculty, no special study of nonrespondents was conducted.

Appendix B. Questionnaires

American College Testing Program

THE INSTITUTIONAL SELF-STUDY SERVICE SURVEY

COLLEGE STUDENT FORM

This research instrument is designed to investigate the nature of your college in terms of the opinions of its students. Your responses, along with those of others, will serve to build a composite picture of the college. Most of the questions ask for your evaluations of various aspects of the institution and about the institution's effects on you. Other background items serve to identify important features of the student body. Answers to these questions provide the institution an idea of the nature of its student body and how the needs of its students can be better met.

After these surveys are completed, ACT will prepare a research report that can aid administrators in educational planning. The report will summarize student's feelings about aspects of the college and the effectiveness of its programs.

The research analysis will relate information on this survey with information collected when you wrote the ACT tests. Such a comparison enables the college to consider what happens to its students after they enroll, in terms of their characteristics upon entering college. To identify yourself for this comparison, you are requested to record your Social Security number on the answer sheet by darkening the proper ovals. Please be assured that your reply to this form is confidential. Identification information is necessary *only* for this research purpose.

The Institutional Self-Study Service is a Research Service to help colleges and Universities add student evaluation as a part of their overall institutional assessment.

INSTITUTIONAL SELF-STUDY SERVICE

Education Fields

Counseling and Guidance	01
Education Administration	02
Elementary Education	03
Physical Education	04
Secondary Education	05
Special Education	06
Education, Other Specialties	07

Social Science and Religious Fields

History	08
Home Economics	09
Dietetics	10
Library and Archival Science	11
Psychology	12
Social Work	13
Sociology	14
Theology and Religion	15
Social Science	
Area Studies	16
American Civilization	17
American Studies	18

Business, Political, and Persuasive Fields

Accounting	19
Advertising	20
Business Administration (4 years)	21
Business and Commerce (2 years)	22
Data Processing	23
Economics	24
Finance	25
Industrial Relations	26
Law	27
Merchandising and Sales	28
Military	29
Political Science, Government, or Public Administration	30
Foreign Services	31
International Relations	32
Public Relations	33
Secretarial Science	34

Scientific Fields

Anatomy	35
Anthropology	36
Archaeology	37
Astronomy	38
Biology or Genetics	39
Botany	40
Chemistry	41
Geography	42
Geology or Geophysics	43
Mathematics or Statistics	44
Meteorology	45
Oceanography	46
Physics	47
Physiology	48
Zoology or Entomology	49

Agriculture and Forestry

Agriculture	50
Fish and Game Management	51
Forestry	52
Soil Conservation	53

Health Fields

Arts and Humanities

Engineering

Trade, Industrial, and Technical

Aviation	90
Construction	91
Drafting	92
Electricity and Electronics	93
Industrial Arts	94
Metal and Machine	95
Mechanical	96
Other Trade	97

My future field of training is not included in the fields
   listed above   98

Housewife   99

Undecided   00

Dear Student:*

We want to know how students view our college. Therefore, you have been specially selected to help us by answering some questions. We have joined other community and junior colleges across the country in a nationwide study called Project Focus. Your answers will be combined with those of other students here and at the other colleges in this major undertaking. Although we are asking you to record your social security number, it is only for record keeping to tell us who answered the questions and who did not. Why should you take the time to answer the questions? First, here is a chance to report your views to us in a systematic way. Secondly, not every student will receive this opportunity, so we are counting on you to represent other students.

The instructions to the materials are outlined below; please follow them carefully so your answers to the questions are properly recorded. . . .

3. Instead of answering Items 25 and 28 on pages 4 and 5 of the printed questionnaire respectively, please respond to the following items. So you will remember to ignore the 2 items, we suggest that you cross out Items 25 and 28 in the printed questionnaire, then mark your answer to each of the following questions in the appropriate space on the answer sheet.

* The following excerpt was taken from a set of supplemental instructions distributed by the campus coordinator to each respondent.

25. What do you estimate your parent's income to be? (Indicate total income before taxes.)

Less than $3,000 per year	0
$3,000 to $4,999	1
$5,000 to $7,499	2
$7,500 to $9,999	3
$10,000 to $14,999	4
$15,000 to $19,999	5
$20,000 to $24,999	6
$25,000 and over	7
I don't know or consider this confidential	8

28. It is clear that students from different racial and ethnic backgrounds often have different educational needs and goals. To understand the differences on our campus it is important for you to assist us by responding to this item. If your background is listed below, and you wish to identify yourself, please respond to this item. *You are not required to provide this information.*

Afro-American	1
American Indian	2
Caucasian/White	3
Mexican/Spanish American	4
Oriental American	5
I prefer not to respond	6

. . .

Thank you for your assistance.

SURVEY QUESTIONNAIRE, COLLEGE STUDENT FORM

Use No. 2 lead pencil. Mark all answers on the separate answer sheet.

1. From the list on the left page, identify your major field. Mark the appropriate code number on your answer sheet. (The top row of ovals is for the tens digit, and the bottom row is for the units digit.) Indicate *only one* field. If you are undecided, mark "00" on your answer sheet and go on to the next question.

2. From the list on the left page, find the best description of your future vocation, and mark its code on your answer sheet. (The top row of ovals is for the tens digit, and the bottom row is for the units digit.) Again, if you are undecided about your future vocation, mark "00" on your answer sheet. If your future vocation is not included in these fields, mark "98" on your answer sheet; or if you anticipate your future vocation to be exclusively that of housewife, mark "99" on your answer sheet and skip Question 3.

3. Which of the following alternatives describes the main role you expect to play in your future vocation? (For example, if you want to be a physicist and work primarily as a researcher, you would mark "1." If you want to be a doctor who specializes in private practice, you would mark "5." An engineering major who plans to become a sales engineer should mark "4." A teacher who wants to become a principal should mark "3." An art major who plans to become a professional artist should mark "5," etc.)

Researcher or investigator	1
Teacher or therapist	2
Administrator or supervisor	3
Promotor or salesman of services or products	4
Practitioner, performer, or producer of services or products	5
None of the above	6
Two or more roles	7
Don't know or undecided	8

4. What is the highest level of education you expect to complete?

Vocational or technical program (less than two years)	0
Junior college degree	1
Bachelor's degree or equivalent	2
One or two years of graduate or professional study (MA, MBA, etc.)	3
Doctor of Philosophy or Doctor of Education (PhD or EdD)	4
Doctor of Medicine (MD)	5
Doctor of Dental Surgery (DDS)	6
Law Degree (LLB, JD)	7

Go to the next page

Theology Degree (BD, THM)   8
Other   9

5. Which *one* of the following statements applies to you?

I do not have a major   0

I have *never* changed my major since entering college:
   (a) and I intend to continue in my present major field   1
   (b) but I intend to change my major in the future   2
   (c) but I would like to change my major, even though I
      do not feel that I should   3
I have changed my major *once* since entering college:
   (a) and I plan to continue in my present major   4
   (b) but I will probably change my major again   5
I have changed my major *twice* since entering college:
   (a) and I plan to continue in my present major   6
   (b) but I will probably change my major again   7
I have changed my major *three or more times* since
   entering college:
   (a) and I plan to continue in my present major   8
   (b) but I will probably change my major again   9

6. When did you make your *present* choice of vocation?

At the present time, I am undecided about my vocation   1
Before high school   2
During high school   3
During my freshman year in college   4
During my sophomore year in college   5
During my junior year in college   6
During my senior year in college   7
After my senior year in college   8

7. Where did you live when you applied for admission to this college?

In the same state as this college and:
   less than 10 miles from the college   0
   10-50 miles from the college   1
   50-100 miles from the college   2
   more than 100 miles from the college   3

In a state adjoining this state and:

less than 50 miles from the college	4
50-100 miles from the college	5
more than 100 miles from the college	6

In a state not adjoining this state	7

In a foreign country:

with an English language background	8
with a non-English language background	9

8. How old are you?

17 or under	1
18	2
19-20	3
21-24	4
25-29	5
30-34	6
35-39	7
40-49	8
50 or over	9

9. Marital or Dating Status:

Single and not going steady	1
Going steady	2
Engaged	3
Married with no children	4
Married with children	5
Separated	6
Divorced	7
Widowed	8
Other	9

10. Father's Occupation:

Managerial or executive (business executive, banker, store manager, etc.)	1
Professional (doctor, lawyer, professor)	2
Sales (auto salesman, department store clerk, etc.)	3
Semiprofessional or technical (programmer, lab technician, etc.)	4
Semiskilled (machine operator, construction worker, etc.)	5

Go to the next page

Skilled trades (electrician, carpenter, plumber, etc.)   6
Small business owner or farm owner   7
Supervisor or public official (office manager, policeman,
    etc.)   8
Unskilled (general laborer, farm laborer, etc.)   9

11. Father's Education:

Less than eighth grade   1
Eighth grade   2
Some high school   3
High school graduate   4
Technical or business, etc.   5
Some college   6
College graduate   7
Some graduate or professional work   8
Received an advanced degree   9

12. Mother's Education:

Less than eighth grade   1
Eighth grade   2
Some high school   3
High school graduate   4
Technical or business, etc.   5
Some college   6
College graduate   7
Some graduate or professional work   8
Received an advanced degree   9

13. Which of the sources of funds listed below has been the *most* important in financing your college work?

Support from my parents or family   1
Support from my spouse   2
Employment or personal savings   3
NDEA loan, bank loan, or other loan   4
Economic Opportunity Grant or Work-Study program   5
GI Bill, ROTC, veterans or social security benefits or
    governmental aid   6
Scholarship, fellowship, or grant   7
Other   8

14. Parents are:

Married	1
Both deceased	2
Father deceased	3
Mother deceased	4
Separated or divorced	5

15. Which *one* of the following statements is true concerning the number of children in your family?

I was an *only* child	1
I was the *younger* of:	
2 children of the same sex	2
2 children of the opposite sex	3
I was the *youngest* of 3 or more children	4
I was the *older* of:	
2 children of the same sex	5
2 children of the opposite sex	6
I was the *oldest* of 3 or more children	7
I was *neither the youngest nor the oldest of:*	
3 or 4 children	8
5 or more children	9

16. How adequate do you feel your high school education was?

Excellent	1
Good	2
Average	3
Below average	4
Very inadequate	5

17. What income (not including that of your spouse) do you expect to have 10 years after graduation?

None since I intend to be a housewife	1
Less than $5,000 as a housewife working part time	2
Less than $7,000 (working full time)	3
$7,000-$8,999	4
$9,000-$10,999	5
$11,000-$14,999	6
$15,000-$24,999	7
$25,000-$49,999	8
over $50,000	9

Go to the next page

18. How satisfied are you with this college as a whole?

Completely satisfied	1
Satisfied	2
Indifferent	3
Unsatisfied	4
Completely unsatisfied	5

19. How well did you apply yourself in high school, and how well have you applied yourself in college?

Less than average in both high school and college	1
Less than average in high school, but average or more than average in college	2
An average amount in both high school and college	3
More than average in high school, but average or less than average in college	4
More than average in both high school and college	5

20. How many times did you move or change schools through elementary school and high school? (Count the change from elementary to junior high or junior high to high school *only if* you moved to a different community.)

None	1
Once	2
2-3 times	3
4-5 times	4
6 or more times	5

21. From what kind of high school or secondary school did you graduate?

Public high school	1
Private, nonreligious, nonmilitary	2
Protestant denominational	3
Catholic	4
Other	5

22. About how many students were in your high school graduating class?

Fewer than 25	1
25-99	2

100-199	3
200-399	4
400-599	5
600-899	6
900 or more	7

23. Which of the following best describes the community that you thought of as your hometown during high school days?

Farm or open county	1
Town or city of:	
less than 500 population	2
501-1,999	3
2,000-9,999	4
10,000-49,999	5
Metropolitan area of	
50,000-249,999 population	6
250,000-499,999	7
500,000-999,999	8
More than 1 million	9

24. About how many hours per week have you usually worked at a part-time job while attending college? (*Exclude* summer work)

Zero	1
1-5	2
6-14	3
15-24	4
25 or more	5

25. About how many hours outside of class per week have you usually studied while attending college?

0-3	1
4-6	2
7-9	3
10-12	4
13-15	5
16-20	6
21-25	7
over 25	8

Go to the next page

26. About how many hours of credit have you averaged per semester (quarter, trimester, etc.) since entering this college?

1-3	1
4-6	2
7-9	3
10-12	4
13-15	5
16-18	6
over 18	7

27. What is your present college residence?

College dormitory	1
Fraternity or sorority house	2
College apartment	3
Off-campus apartment	4
Off-campus room	5
At home with parents	6
Other	7

28. Have you transferred to this college from another college?

No	1
Yes, from a *two-year* college:	
prior to this school year	2
at the beginning of or during this school year	3
Yes, from a *private liberal-arts* college:	
prior to this school year	4
at the beginning of or during this school year	5
Yes, from a *state* university or public four-year college:	
prior to this school year	6
at the beginning of or during this school year	7
Yes, from *some other* higher education institution:	
prior to this school year	8
at the beginning of or during this school year	9

Questions 29-40 describe possible college goals of students. Indicate the degree of importance you attach to each goal by using the following code:

Essential (*a goal you feel you must accomplish*)	1
Very important	2

Desirable (*a goal of some importance, but less vital than those
rated 1 or 2*)   3
Not important (*a goal of little or no importance*)   4

Be sure to respond to every question.

29. To improve my ability to think and reason.
30. To broaden my intellectual interests and my understanding of the world.
31. To increase my appreciation of art, music, literature, and other cultural expressions.
32. To discover my vocational interests.
33. To attain specific skills that will be useful on a job.
34. To meet the academic requirements necessary to enter a profession.
35. To increase my effectiveness in interpersonal relations.
36. To learn how to be an effective leader.
37. To become more capable and interesting socially.
38. To learn how to deal with political or social injustice.
39. To develop more personal independence and self-reliance.
40. To find a cause or causes I can really believe in.

A number of college policies, practices, or facilities are described in questions 41-58 below. Indicate your opinion of these as they apply to your college by using the following code:

Agree   1
Partly agree and partly disagree   2
Disagree   3
I have no opinion on the matter   N

41. There is adequate provision for student privacy.
42. The regulations governing student conduct are constructive.
43. Rules governing the invitation of controversial speakers are reasonable.
44. The campus newspaper gives a balanced presentation to controversial events.
45. Laboratory facilities for the physical sciences are adequate.
46. Laboratory facilities for the biological sciences are adequate.
47. The cultural program (lectures, concerts, exhibits, plays) is satisfactory in terms of quality and quantity.
48. Sufficient recreational opportunities and facilities (bowling, swimming, etc.) are available.

Go to the next page

49. Regulations governing academic probation and dismissal are sensible.
50. Examinations are usually thorough and fair.
51. Library materials are easily accessible.
52. Instructors are generally available for assistance with classwork.
53. Adequate provision is made for gifted students (e.g., honors program, independent study, undergraduate research, etc.)
54. Students have ample opportunity to participate in college policy-making.
55. The college social program (dances, parties, etc.) is successful.
56. Housing regulations (living in apartments, off-campus rooms, etc.) are reasonable.
57. Disciplinary procedures and policies are fair.
58. College food services are adequate in terms of quality, cost, and efficiency.

Questions 59-67 refer to services which are frequently provided by colleges. Describe your reaction to these services at your college by using the following code:

The service was extremely valuable to me	1
I found the service to be worthwhile	2
I received little benefit from the service	3
I've never used this service	4
Our college does not offer this service	5

59. Academic advising service (assistance in selecting courses, adjusting schedules, planning programs, etc.).
60. Counseling service (assistance in choosing a major, vocational planning, resolving personal problems, etc.).
61. Financial needs service (assistance in obtaining a scholarship, loan, part time job, or assistance in budgeting and controlling expenses).
62. Extracurricular activities assistance (in getting started in activities or in making the most of extracurricular opportunities).
63. Orientation service (assistance in getting started in college—learning the ropes, getting acquainted, overcoming apprehensions).
64. Housing services (assistance in locating suitable housing).
65. Housing advisory services (assistance in dealing with roommate problems, advice in handling everyday concerns, programs designed to make the housing arrangement more educational and enjoyable).

66. Health service (assistance in dealing with illness or injury).
67. Developmental education services (improvement of reading, study skills, spelling, etc.).

Questions 68-79 below list some statements describing possible outcomes of a college education. Indicate the degree to which you feel you have made progress on each of these outcomes by marking your answer sheet in accordance with the following code:

Substantial progress	1
Some progress	2
Not much progress	3

68. Acquiring a broad cultural and literary education.
69. Acquiring vocational training—skills and techniques directly applicable to a job.
70. Acquiring background and specialization for further education in some professional, scientific, or scholarly field.
71. Understanding different philosophies, cultures, and ways of life.
72. Social development—gaining experience and skill in relating to other people.
73. Personal development—understanding one's abilities and limitations, interests and standards of behavior.
74. Knowing how to participate effectively as a citizen in one's community and in wider areas.
75. Developing an ability to write and to speak clearly, correctly, and effectively.
76. Developing an ability to think critically and to understand the origin, nature, and limitations of knowledge.
77. Developing an appreciation and an enjoyment of art, music, and literature.
78. Developing an understanding and an appreciation of science and technology.
79. Improving prospects for making high income and gaining professional status.

Questions 80-93 ask you to describe the instructors you have had at this college. Use the following scale to indicate how frequently each statement is true:

A majority of my instructors	1
About half of my instructors	2
A minority of my instructors	3

Go to the next page

80. Instructors give students ample opportunity to participate in discussion, to ask questions, and to express points of view.
81. Lectures are dry, dull, and monotonous.
82. Students are given an important voice in determining class objectives and procedures.
83. Instructors appear to be uneasy and nervous.
84. Faculty members have an unusual facility for communicating their knowledge to students.
85. Instructors criticize or embarrass students in the classroom.
86. Instructors present material in an entertaining (e.g., dramatic, humorous) manner.
87. Instructors give disorganized, superficial, or imprecise treatment to their material.
88. Instructors give personal opinions or describe personal experiences.
89. Instructors don't seem to care whether or not class material is understood.
90. Out-of-class assignments (reading, papers, etc.) are reasonable in length.
91. Insufficient distinction is made between major ideas and less important details.
92. Instructors relate course material to contemporary problems.
93. Instructors seem to be "out of touch" with student life.

Questions 94-123 refer to your use of leisure time while you have been attending college. If, while attending college, you have engaged in the activity ON YOUR OWN, i.e., NOT AS A PART OF A CLASS ASSIGNMENT, mark the Y ("Yes") response. If you cannot recall having participated in the activity while in college (except, perhaps, as part of an assignment), mark the N ("No") response.

94. Attempted to invent something.
95. Read some poetry.
96. Discussed merits of political-economic systems (e.g., communism, socialism) with friends.
97. Attended a scientific lecture.
98. Visited an art exhibit.
99. Discussed world or national political problems (candidates, issues) with friends.
100. Attended a scientific exhibit.
101. Tried some sketching, drawing, or painting.
102. Watched four or more TV news specials in a year.

103. Read a technical journal or a scientific article.
104. Attended a poetry reading or a literary talk.
105. Discussed social issues (e.g., civil rights, pacifism) with friends.
106. Attempted to solve mathematical puzzles.
107. Attended a stage play.
108. Discussed campus issues with friends.
109. Attempted to develop a new scientific theory.
110. Read six or more articles a year in *Atlantic, Commonweal, Harpers*, and/or *Saturday Review.*
111. Attended a lecture on a current social, economic, or political problem.
112. Discussed a scientific theory or event with friends.
113. Discussed art or music with friends.
114. Read the editorial column of a newspaper at least once a week.
115. Devised a mathematical puzzle.
116. Discussed philosophy or religion with friends.
117. Read an article or book analyzing in depth a political or social issue.
118. Regularly read popular accounts of scientific advances (in *Time, Newsweek*, etc.).
119. Discussed plays, novels, or poetry with friends.
120. Read a biography or autobiography of a political or social reform leader.
121. Explained or illustrated a scientific principle to someone.
122. Attended a music recital or concert.
123. Read a book on psychology, sociology, or history.

Questions 124-223 also deal with experiences you may have had in college. They are grouped into ten lists of "out-of-class" accomplishments (Leadership, Social Participation, etc.); each list contains ten items which describe specific accomplishments or awards.
For each of the lists, read all ten items and then indicate which ones are true of you by blackening the appropriate oval or ovals on your answer sheet. If on a given list none of the ten items are true for you, blacken the "None" oval and go on to the next list.
Don't be discouraged by these statements; only an unusual student will be able to say "Yes" to many items.

LIST 1. LEADERSHIP

124. Elected to one or more student offices.
125. Appointed to one or more student offices.

Go to the next page

126. Was an active member of four or more student groups.
127. Elected president of class (freshman, sophomore, etc.) in any year of college.
128. Served on a student-faculty committee or group.
129. Elected or appointed as a member of a campus-wide student group, such as student council, student senate, etc.
130. Served on a governing board or an executive council of a student group.
131. Elected as one of the officers of a class (freshman, sophomore, etc.) in any year of college.
132. Elected president of a "special interest" student club, such as psychology club, mountain climbing club, etc.
133. Received an award or special recognition of any kind for leadership.

LIST 2. SOCIAL PARTICIPATION

134. Actively campaigned to elect another student to a campus office.
135. Organized a college political group or campaign.
136. Worked actively in an off-campus political campaign.
137. Worked actively in a student movement to change institutional rules, procedures, or policies.
138. Initiated or organized a student movement to change institutional rules, procedures, or policies.
139. Participated in a student political group (Young Democrats, Young Republicans, etc.).
140. Participated in one or more demonstrations for some political or social goal, such as civil rights, free speech for students, states' rights, etc.
141. Wrote a "letter to the editor" regarding a social or civic problem.
142. Wrote a letter to a state legislator or U.S. representative or senator about pending or proposed legislation.
143. Worked actively in a special study group (other than a class assignment) for the investigation of a social or political issue.

LIST 3. ART

144. Won a prize or award in art competition (drawing, painting, sculpture, ceramics, architecture, etc.).
145. Exhibited or published at my college one or more works of art, such as drawings, paintings, sculptures, ceramics, etc.

146. Had drawings, photographs, or other art work published in a public newspaper or magazine.
147. Entered an artistic competition of any kind.
148. Produced on my own (not as part of a course) one or more works of art, such as drawings, paintings, sculptures, ceramics, etc.
149. Exhibited or published *not at my college* one or more works of art, such as drawing, paintings, sculptures, ceramics, etc.
150. Sold one or more works of art, such as drawings, paintings, sculptures, ceramics, etc.
151. Own a collection of art books, paintings, or reproductions.
152. Designed, made, and sold handicraft items such as jewelry, leathercrafts, etc.
153. Created or designed election posters, program covers, greeting cards, stage settings for a play, etc.

LIST 4. SOCIAL SERVICE

154. Worked actively in a student service group or organization.
155. Worked actively in a charity drive.
156. Worked as a volunteer aide in a hospital, clinic, or home.
157. Served as a big brother (sister) or advisor to one or more foreign students.
158. Organized a student service group.
159. Worked actively in an off-campus service group or organization.
160. Worked as a volunteer on a campus or civic improvement project.
161. Participated in a program to assist children or adults who were handicapped mentally, physically, or economically.
162. Voluntarily tutored a fellow student.
163. Received an award or recognition for any kind of campus or community service.

LIST 5. SCIENTIFIC

164. Built scientific equipment (laboratory apparatus, a computer, etc.) on my own (not as a part of a course).
165. Was appointed a teaching or research assistant in a scientific field.
166. Received a prize or award for a scientific paper or project.
167. Gave an original paper at a convention or meeting sponsored by a scientific society or association.

Go to the next page

168. On my own (not as part of a course), carried out or repeated one or more scientific experiments, recorded scientific observations of things or events in the natural setting, or assembled and maintained a collection of scientific specimens.
169. Authored or co-authored scientific or scholarly paper published (or in press) in a scientific journal.
170. Invented a patentable device.
171. Was a member of a student honorary scientific society.
172. Entered a scientific competition of any kind.
173. Wrote an unpublished scientific paper (not a course assignment).

LIST 6. HUMANISTIC-CULTURAL

174. Developed and followed a program of reading of poetry, novels, biographies, etc. on my own (not course assignment).
175. Was a member of a student honorary society in the humanities (literature, philosophy, language, etc.).
176. Built a personal library around a core collection of poetry, novels, biographies, etc.
177. Attended a convention or meeting of a scholarly society in the humanities (literature, philosophy, language, etc.).
178. Authored or co-authored an original paper published (or in press) in a scholarly journal in the humanities (literature, philosophy, language, etc.).
179. Read scholarly journals in the humanities on my own (not as a course assignment).
180. Read one or more "classic" literary works on my own (not as a course assignment).
181. Wrote on my own (not a course assignment) an unpublished scholarly paper in the humanities.
182. Won a prize or award for work in the humanities.
183. Gave an original paper at a convention or meeting sponsored by a scholarly society in the humanities.

LIST 7. RELIGIOUS SERVICE

184. Was an active member of a student religious group.
185. Organized or reorganized a student religious group.
186. Was an active member of an off-campus religious group (not a church).
187. Held one or more offices in a religious organization.

188. Led one or more religious services.
189. Taught in a church, synagogue, etc.
190. Attended one or more religious retreats, conferences, etc.
191. Participated in a religious study group.
192. Worked to raise money for a religious institution or group.
193. Did voluntary work for a religious institution or group.

LIST 8. MUSIC

194. Composed or arranged music which was publicly performed.
195. Publicly performed on two or more musical instruments (including voice) which do not belong to the same family of instruments.
196. Conducted music which was publicly performed.
197. Presented in public a solo recital which was not under the auspices of a college or church.
198. Attained recognition in the form of an award or scholarship in a national or international music competition.
199. Received pay for performing as a professional music teacher on a continuing basis.
200. Composed or arranged music which has been published.
201. Attained a first division rating in a state or regional solo music contest.
202. Received pay for performing as a professional musician on a continuing basis.
203. Authored or co-authored a book, an article, or a criticism bearing on the general subject of music.

LIST 9. WRITING

204. Had poems, stories, essays, or articles published in a public (not college) newspaper, anthology, etc.
205. Wrote one or more plays (including radio or TV plays) which were given public performance.
206. Was feature writer, reporter, etc., for college paper, annual, magazine, anthology, etc.
207. Was editor for college paper, annual, magazine, anthology, etc.
208. Did news or feature writing for public (not college) newspaper.
209. Had poems, stories, essays, or articles published in a college publication.
210. Wrote an original but unpublished piece of creative writing on my own (not as part of a course).

Go to the next page

211. Won a literary prize or award for creative writing.
212. Systematically recorded my observations and thoughts in a diary or journal as resource material for writing.
213. Was a member of a student honorary group in creative writing or journalism.

LIST 10. SPEECH AND DRAMA

214. Participated in one or more contests in speech, debate, extemporaneous speaking, etc.
215. Placed second, third, or fourth in a contest in speech, debate, extemporaneous speaking, etc.
216. Won one or more contests in speech, debate, extemporaneous speaking, etc.
217. Had one or more minor roles in plays produced by my college or university.
218. Had one or more leads in plays produced by my college or university.
219. Had one or more leads or minor roles in plays *not* produced by my university.
220. Gave dramatic performance on radio or TV program.
221. Received an award for acting or other phase of drama.
222. Gave a recital in speech.
223. Participated in a poetry reading, play reading, dramatic production, etc. (not a course assignment).

Items 224-247 on your answer sheet provide the opportunity to answer relevant questions designed by your college to meet special needs on your campus.

COLLEGE STUDENT FORM SUPPLEMENT*

Items 224-247 provide you with the opportunity to comment on the goals or purposes of your college. How important are these goals? Many of the more commonly mentioned goals are listed in the questions that follow. Some may be thought of as "output" or "ultimate" goals while others are more appropriately classified as "support" or "maintenance" goals. In these questions, both types are

*From *Institutional Goals Inventory*. A preliminary form developed for research purposes by Educational Testing Service. Copyright © 1970 by Educational Testing Service. All rights reserved. Adapted and reproduced by permission.

considered important. For each statement of goal in Items 224-235 indicate how much emphasis in your opinion is being placed on the goal at your institution at the present time using the following codes (Mark your answer on the answer sheet.):

1 = Emphasized Very Strongly
2 = Emphasized Strongly
3 = Emphasized a Little
4 = Emphasized Hardly at All
5 = Emphasized Not at All

224. To help formulate programs in a number of public policy areas such as pollution control, urban renewal, and health care.
225. To ensure student participation in institutional decision-making.
226. To make special efforts to attract faculty members who are also members of groups that are in the minority on this campus.
227. To help students acquire the ability to adapt to new occupational requirements as technology and society change.
228. To ensure faculty participation in institutional decision-making.
229. To provide some form of education for any student, regardless of his academic ability.
230. To allocate percentages of the total enrollment for minority groups or groups having low socioeconomic status.
231. To help students develop a respect for their own ability and an understanding of their limitations.
232. To be responsive to the needs of the local community.
233. To provide an opportunity for re-educating and retraining those whose vocational capabilities have become obsolete.
234. To make financial assistance available to any student who wants to enroll in college.
235. To serve the higher education needs of youth from the surrounding community.

For each statement of goal in Items 236-247 indicate how important each goal should be at your institution during the coming decade using the code:

1 = Of Extremely High Importance
2 = Of High Importance

Go to the next page

3 = Of Medium Importance
4 = Of Low Importance
5 = Of No Importance

236. To help formulate programs in a number of public policy areas such as pollution control, urban renewal, and health care.
237. To ensure student participation in institutional decision-making.
238. To make special efforts to attract faculty members who are also members of groups that are in the minority on this campus.
239. To help students acquire the ability to adapt to new occupational requirements as technology and society change.
240. To ensure faculty participation in institutional decision-making.
241. To provide some form of education for any student, regardless of his academic ability.
242. To allocate percentages of the total enrollment for minority groups or groups having low socioeconomic status.
243. To help students develop a respect for their own ability and an understanding of their limitations.
244. To be responsive to the needs of the local community.
245. To provide an opportunity for re-education and retraining those whose vocational capabilities have become obsolete.
246. To make financial assistance available to any student who wants to enroll in college.
247. To serve the higher education needs of youth from the surrounding community.

Exhibit II

Project Focus Faculty Questionnaire

March 1971

Dear Colleague:

Your college is cooperating in a national study of the nation's community and junior colleges being conducted by the American Association of Junior Colleges (AAJC) and funded by the W. K. Kellogg Foundation. Its aim is to examine the long-range goals and present practices of the community-junior colleges and, in the process, to identify the social and economic trends which will influence their role and function for the coming decade.

As faculty members, we are interested in your background and perceptions as to the future of community-junior colleges. Since you are a very select sample and you will be representing the views of other faculty members, it is important that you respond to this questionnaire.

Your answers will be kept completely confidential. No one will see your responses except the professional staff working on this project. All results will be summarized by groups; individual responses will not be released. However, for the purpose of monitoring question-naire returns, we need your name on the answer sheet.

The following pages contain the instructions for recording your answers and the questions to be answered.

Sincerely,

E. J. Gleazer, Jr.
Project Director

. . .

INSTITUTIONAL SELF-STUDY SERVICE

Education Fields

Counseling and Guidance	01
Education Administration	02
Elementary Education	03
Physical Education	04
Secondary Education	05
Special Education	06
Education, Other Specialties	07

Social Science and Religious Fields

History	08
Home Economics	09
Dietetics	10
Library and Archival Science	11
Psychology	12
Social Work	13
Sociology	14
Theology and Religion	15
Social Science	
Area Studies	16
American Civilization	17
American Studies	18

Business, Political, and Persuasive Fields

Accounting	19
Advertising	20
Business Administration (4 years)	21
Business and Commerce (2 years)	22
Data Processing	23
Economics	24
Finance	25
Industrial Relations	26
Law	27
Merchandising and Sales	28
Military	29
Political Science, Government, or Public Administration	30
Foreign Services	31
International Relations	32
Public Relations	33
Secretarial Science	34

Scientific Fields

Agriculture and Forestry

Health Fields

Arts and Humanities

Creative Writing	69
Drama and Theater	70
English and English Literature	71
Foreign Language and Literature	72
Journalism	73
Music	74
Philosophy	75
Radio-TV Communications	76
Speech	77
General Education or Liberal Arts (2 years)	78
Other Arts and Humanities	79

Engineering

Aeronautical	80
Agricultural	81
Architectural	82
Automotive	83
Chemical or Nuclear	84
Civil	85
Electrical or Electronic	86
Industrial	87
Mechanical	88
Other	89

Trade, Industrial, and Technical

Aviation	90
Construction	91
Drafting	92
Electricity and Electronics	93
Industrial Arts	94
Metal and Machine	95
Mechanical	96
Other Trade	97

**My future field of training is not included in the fields
   listed above**   98

Housewife   99

Undecided   00

1. From the list on the left page find the name of the field which comes closest to your departmental affiliation. Enter the code number of the field on the answer sheet. (The top row of rectangles is for the tens digit and the bottom row is for the units digit.)
2. From the list on the left page find the name of the field in which you received your highest degree. Enter the code number of the field on the answer sheet. (The top row of rectangles is for the tens digit and the bottom row is for the units digit.)
3. Much has been written about the differences in educational philosophy and approaches of faculty members from different backgrounds. To investigate the differences, indeed to determine if there are any, we are asking you to indicate your racial and ethnic background. If you wish to identify your background and if it is listed below, please respond to this item. *You are not required to respond to this item.*

Afro-American/Black	1
American Indian	2
Caucasian/White	3
Mexican/Spanish-American	4
Oriental American	5
Other	6
I prefer not to respond	7

4. and 5. How many class hours or periods do you spend each week. in actual student instruction (e.g., 30 hours for 5, 6-period days; 12 hours for 3-hour courses). Enter 2 digits—the tens digit beside 4 (zero if appropriate) and units digit beside 5.
6. If you were employed by an educational institution immediately prior to being employed by your current institution, which of the following best describes it? Omit if not employed by educational institution and go to Item 7.

Elementary school	1
Junior high school	2
Comprehensive high school	3
Vocational, technical high school	4
Technical institute, area center	5
Junior, community college	6
Four-year college, university	7
Other	8

Go to the next page

Using the code below, indicate the number of calendar years you were employed by the institutions listed in Items 7-12.

Never employed	omit
1-4 years	1
5-9 years	2
10-14 years	3
15-19 years	4
20-24 years	5
25-29 years	6
30-34 years	7
35-39 years	8
40 or more years	9

7. Elementary school or junior high school
8. Comprehensive high school
9. Vocational, technical high school
10. Technical institute, area center
11. Junior, community college
12. Four-year college, university
13. Counting this year, how many years have you taught in educational institutions in all?

1-5 years	1
6-10 years	2
11-15 years	3
16-20 years	4
21-25 years	5
26-30 years	6
31-35 years	7
36 or more years	8

14. Which of the following is the most appropriate description of *your* major job at this institution this semester (spring 1970-71)?

Full-time faculty member	1
Part-time faculty member	2
Part-time faculty member and part-time counselor	3
Part-time faculty member and part-time administrator	4
Other	5

15. Which of the following is the worst aspect of teaching?

   1. A teacher is expected to spend an undue amount of time in community, social, and extracurricular activities.
   2. Poor physical conditions in which to work.
   3. Educational personnel are held unjustly responsible for community and family shortcomings in child rearing.
   4. Unappreciative and unmotivated student.
   5. Poor administration and excessive red tape.
   6. Heavy teaching loads.
   7. Burden of excessive clerical and administrative work.
   8. Not enough time during regular school hours to do adequate background preparation or keep up to date.
   9. No particular drawbacks.

16. How satisfied are you with this college as a whole?

Completely satisfied	1
Satisfied	2
Indifferent	3
Unsatisfied	4
Completely unsatisfied	5

If you expect that your major occupation will be in the field of education 5 years from now, answer Questions 18 and 19. Otherwise, answer Question 17.

17. Since you do not expect that your *major* occupation will be in the field of education 5 years from now, what is likely to be your major activity?

Marriage, raising family	1
Work in private business or industry	2
Work in government	3
Self-employed	4
Retirement	5
Other	6
Undecided	7

Go on to question 20.

Go to the next page

18. In what area of education do you expect to be in 5 years from
    now?

    Teaching   1
    Counseling   2
    Administration   3
    Other   4

19. What type of school do you expect to be in 5 years from now?

    High school   1
    Vocational, technical center   2
    Junior, community college   3
    College, university   4
    Other   5

20. What is the highest degree you hold?

    High school diploma   1
    A.A., A.A.S., A.S.   2
    B.A., B.S., B.Ed.   3
    M.A., M.S., M.Ed.   4
    Ph.D., Ed.D.   5

21. Which of the following degrees are you now working on? (If
    none, omit.)

    High school diploma   1
    A.A., A.A.S., A.S.   2
    B.A., B.S., B.Ed.   3
    M.A., M.S., M.Ed.   4
    PhD., Ed.D.   5

Skip Questions 22-40. Therefore, begin answering the following
questions beginning with Item 41.
A number of college policies, practices, or facilities are described in
Questions 41-58 below. Indicate your opinion of these as they apply
to your college by using the following code:

    Agree   1
    Partly agree and partly disagree   2
    Disagree   3
    I have no opinion on the matter   N

41. There is adequate provision for student privacy. (Remember to record your opinion beside *41* on answer sheet.)
42. The regulations governing student conduct are constructive.
43. Rules governing the invitation of controversial speakers are reasonable.
44. The campus newspaper gives a balanced presentation to controversial events.
45. Laboratory facilities for the physical sciences are adequate.
46. Laboratory facilities for the biological sciences are adequate.
47. The cultural program (lectures, concerts, exhibits, plays) is satisfactory in terms of quality and quantity.
48. Sufficient recreational opportunities and facilities (bowling, swimming, etc.) are available.
49. Regulations governing academic probation and dismissal are sensible.
50. Examinations are usually thorough and fair.
51. Library materials are easily accessible.
52. Instructors are generally available for assistance with classwork.
53. Adequate provision is made for gifted students (e.g., honors program, independent study, undergraduate research, etc.)
54. Students have ample opportunity to participate in college policy-making.
55. The college social program (dances, parties, etc.) is successful.
56. Housing regulations (living in apartments, off-campus rooms, etc.) are reasonable.
57. Disciplinary procedures and policies are fair.
58. College food services are adequate in terms of quality, cost, and efficiency.

Questions 59-67 refer to services which are frequently provided by colleges. Describe your reaction to these services at this college by using the following code:

This service is extremely valuable to the students	1
This service is worthwhile	2
The students use this service but receive little benefit from it	3
The students never use this service	4
The college does not offer this service	5

59. Academic advising service (assistance in selecting courses, adjusting schedules, planning programs, etc.).
60. Counseling service (assistance in choosing a major, vocational planning, resolving personal problems, etc.)

Go to the next page

61. Financial needs service (assistance in obtaining a scholarship, loan, part-time job, or assistance in budgeting and controlling expenses).
62. Extracurricular activities assistance (in getting started in activities or in making the most of extracurricular opportunities).
63. Orientation service (assistance in getting started in college—leaning the ropes, getting acquainted, overcoming apprehensions).
64. Housing services (assistance in locating suitable housing).
65. Housing advisory services (assistance in dealing with roommate problems, advice in handling everyday concerns, programs designed to make the housing arrangement more educational and enjoyable).
66. Health service (assistance in dealing with illness or injury).
67. Developmental education services (improvement of reading, study skills, spelling, etc.)

Again, we are skipping some questions (68-79). So please be sure to record your answers in the appropriate place on the answer sheet.

Questions 80-93 ask you to describe how you think the typical student sees instructors at this college. Use the following scale to indicate how frequently each statement is true:

A majority of instructors	1
About half of the instructors	2
A minority of instructors	3

80. Instructors give students ample opportunity to participate in discussion, to ask questions, and to express points of view.
81. Lectures are dry, dull, and monotonous.
82. Students are given an important voice in determining class objectives and procedures.
83. Instructors appear to be uneasy and nervous.
84. Faculty members have an unusual facility for communicating their knowledge to students.
85. Instructors criticize or embarrass students in the classroom.
86. Instructors present material in an entertaining (e.g., dramatic, humorous) manner.
87. Instructors give disorganized, superficial, or imprecise treatment to their material.

88. Instructors give personal opinions or describe personal experiences.
89. Instructors don't seem to care whether or not class material is understood.
90. Out-of-class assignments (reading, papers, etc.) are reasonable in length.
91. Insufficient distinction is made between major ideas and less important details.
92. Instructors relate course material to contemporary problems.
93. Instructors seem to be "out of touch" with student life.

Items 94-103 indicate activities you might do during the summer of 1971. Indicate what you plan to do by using the following code:

    Yes Y
    No   N

94. Teach.
95. Develop course plans.
96. Attend summer school.
97. Work full-time at my nonteaching job.
98. Take a summer job related to my teaching field.
99. Take a summer job unrelated to my teaching field.
100. Research, write.
101. Travel.
102. Rest, marriage, be with family.
103. Undecided.

Respond to Questions 104-109 by using the following code:

    Yes Y
    No   N

104. Do you hold a certificate of apprenticeship?
105. Do you hold a certificate of proficiency?
106. Did you receive your highest educational degree from an institution in this state?
107. Do you feel junior colleges should be more selective of their students than they are now?
108. Do you feel junior college faculty members have a harder job than faculty members at 4-year colleges?
109. Do you feel you have a more important job than faculty members at 4-year colleges?

Go to the next page

Once again we are skipping some items. Be sure to record your answers to the questions below on the answer sheet in the proper place.

Faculty Goals Inventory*

Items 224-235 provide you with the opportunity to comment on the goals or purposes of your college. How important are these goals? Many of the more commonly mentioned goals are listed in the questions that follow. Some may be thought of as "output" or "ultimate" goals while others are more appropriately classified as "support" or "maintenance" goals. In these questions, both types are considered important.

For each statement of goal in Items 224-235 indicate how much emphasis is being placed on the goal at your institution at the present time using the following codes (Mark your answer on the answer sheet.):

1 = Emphasized Very Strongly
2 = Emphasized Strongly
3 = Emphasized a Little
4 = Emphasized Hardly at All
5 = Emphasized Not at All

224. To help formulate programs in a number of public policy areas such as pollution control, urban renewal, and health care.
225. To ensure student participation in institutional decision-making.
226. To make special efforts to attract faculty members who are also members of groups that are in the minority on this campus.
227. To help students acquire the ability to adapt to new occupational requirements as technology and society change.
228. To ensure faculty participation in institutional decision-making.

229. To provide some form of education for any student, regardless of his academic ability.
230. To allocate percentages of the total enrollment for minority groups or groups having low socioeconomic status.
231. To help students develop a respect for their own ability and an understanding of their limitations.
232. To be responsive to the needs of the local community.
233. To provide an opportunity for re-educating and retraining those whose vocational capabilities have become obsolete.
234. To make financial assistance available to any student who wants to enroll in college.
235. To serve the higher education needs of youth from the surrounding community.

For each statement of goal in Items 236-247 indicate how important each goal should be at your institution during the coming decade using the code:

1 = Of Extremely High Importance
2 = Of High Importance
3 = Of Medium Importance
4 = Of Low Importance
5 = Of No Importance

236. To help formulate programs in a number of public policy areas such as pollution control, urban renewal, and health care.
237. To ensure student participation in institutional decision-making.
238. To make special efforts to attract faculty members who are also members of groups that are in the minority on this campus.
239. To help students acquire the ability to adapt to new occupational requirements as technology and society change.
240. To ensure faculty participation in institutional decision-making.
241. To provide some form of education for any student, regardless of his academic ability.
242. To allocate percentages of the total enrollment for minority groups or groups having low socioeconomic status.
243. To help students develop a respect for their own ability and an understanding of their limitations.
244. To be responsive to the needs of the local community.

Go to the next page

245. To provide an opportunity for re-educating and retraining those whose vocational capabilities have become obsolete.
246. To make financial assistance available to any student who wants to enroll in college.
247. To service the higher education needs of youth from the surrounding community.

Exhibit III

PROJECT FOCUS STRATEGIES FOR CHANGE

Madison Office Building
Suite 600
1155 15th Street, N.W.
Washington, D.C. 20005

Area Code 202/833-1177

Edmund J. Gleazer, Jr.
Project Director

David S. Bushnell
Research Director

Francis C. Pray
Associate

**COMMUNITY AND JUNIOR COLLEGE
PRESIDENTS' QUESTIONNAIRE**

Attached for your response is a brief questionnaire designed to provide information about the significant goals and practices at your institution. Your responses will become a part of a larger data bank of information to be used in a nationwide study of community and junior colleges. Your responses will be kept strictly confidential and your name and your college will never be associated with your individual answers in any reports. Findings and recommendations of the study will be reported back to you on an aggregate basis in the fall of 1971.

We will appreciate the return of the questionnaire in the enclosed stamped, self-addressed envelope as soon as possible. Please check to see that the information on the address label is correct.

If a question or part of a question does not apply to your institution, please indicate by checking the appropriate response or by writing in "does not apply." Thank you very much for your assistance.

Edmund J. Gleazer, Jr.
Project Director

To Be Filled out by the Campus President Only

A National Study by the American Association of Junior Colleges under a Grant from the W. K. Kellogg Foundation.

1. If your campus financial resources (operating and capital budgets) were to vary over the next 10 years in the indicated manner (assuming that enrollment stayed the same), what priority would you assign to each of the activities listed below? Please circle one response only in each of the three columns for each item listed.

IF FINANCIAL RESOURCES —

Activities	Not applicable at this institution	Decreased substantially			Stayed the same			Increased substantially		
		High priority	Medium priority	Low priority	High priority	Medium priority	Low priority	High priority	Medium priority	Low priority
a. College-sponsored workshops and seminars	0	1	2	3	1	2	3	1	2	3
b. Community service centers (off campus)	0	1	2	3	1	2	3	1	2	3
c. Ethnic studies	0	1	2	3	1	2	3	1	2	3
d. Faculty training programs	0	1	2	3	1	2	3	1	2	3
e. Outreach counseling and recruitment	0	1	2	3	1	2	3	1	2	3
f. Noncredit courses	0	1	2	3	1	2	3	1	2	3
g. Remedial programs	0	1	2	3	1	2	3	1	2	3
h. Residential facilities	0	1	2	3	1	2	3	1	2	3
i. Student extracurricular activities (band, choir, organizations, publications, etc.)	0	1	2	3	1	2	3	1	2	3
j. Adult evening courses	0	1	2	3	1	2	3	1	2	3
k. Student guidance and counseling	0	1	2	3	1	2	3	1	2	3
l. Library services	0	1	2	3	1	2	3	1	2	3
m. Nontenured faculty	0	1	2	3	1	2	3	1	2	3
n. Maintenance	0	1	2	3	1	2	3	1	2	3

2. Colleges serve a number of purposes, some of which may be regarded as more important than others. What do you consider to be the purposes of your institution? How important are these goals? Many of the more commonly mentioned goals of a college are listed in the question below. Some may be thought of as "output" or "ultimate" goals while others are more appropriately classified as "support" or "maintenance" goals. In this question, both types are considered important. Please rate each goal statement in terms of its actual emphasis today and its potential importance in the coming decade (indicate your rating by circling the number under your rating for each goal).

Goal Statement[a]	This Goal Is Presently—					In the Coming Decade, This Goal Should Be—				
	Emphasized very strongly	*Emphasized strongly*	*Emphasized a little*	*Emphasized hardly at all*	*Emphasized not at all*	*Of extremely high importance*	*Of high importance*	*Of medium importance*	*Of low importance*	*Of no importance*
a. To serve the higher education needs of youth from the surrounding community.	1	2	3	4	5	1	2	3	4	5
b. To experiment with new forms of instruction.	1	2	3	4	5	1	2	3	4	5
c. To make available financial assistance so that any academically qualified student is able to enroll and remain in college.	1	2	3	4	5	1	2	3	4	5
d. To increase the desire and ability of students to undertake self-directed study.	1	2	3	4	5	1	2	3	4	5
e. To help formulate programs in a number of public policy areas such as pollution control, urban renewal, and health care.	1	2	3	4	5	1	2	3	4	5
f. To develop educational programs for special categories of students, e.g., disadvantaged, very bright, foreign students, etc.	1	2	3	4	5	1	2	3	4	5
g. To establish and clearly define the purposes the institution will serve.	1	2	3	4	5	1	2	3	4	5
h. To ensure student participation in institutional decision-making.	1	2	3	4	5	1	2	3	4	5
i. To make special efforts to attract faculty members who are also members of groups that are in the minority on this campus.	1	2	3	4	5	1	2	3	4	5
j. To help students acquire the ability to adapt to new occupational requirements as technology and society change.	1	2	3	4	5	1	2	3	4	5

[a] From *Institutional Goals Inventory.* A preliminary form developed for research purposes by Education Testing Service. Copyright © 1970 by Educational Testing Service. All rights reserved. Adapted and reproduced by permission.

continued

Goal Statement	This Goal Is Presently—					In the Coming Decade, This Goal Should Be—				
	Emphasized very strongly	*Emphasized strongly*	*Emphasized a little*	*Emphasized hardly at all*	*Emphasized not at all*	*Of extremely high importance*	*Of high importance*	*Of medium importance*	*Of low importance*	*Of no importance*
k. To maintain an atmosphere of intellectual excitement among faculty, students, and administrators.	1	2	3	4	5	1	2	3	4	5
l. To increase the number and diversity of sources of income.	1	2	3	4	5	1	2	3	4	5
m. To provide an opportunity for re-educating and retraining those whose vocational capabilities have become obsolete.	1	2	3	4	5	1	2	3	4	5
n. To strengthen the religious faith of students.	1	2	3	4	5	1	2	3	4	5
o. To help solve social, economic, or political problems in the immediate geographical area.	1	2	3	4	5	1	2	3	4	5
p. To ensure faculty participation in institutional decision-making.	1	2	3	4	5	1	2	3	4	5
q. To provide some form of education for any student, regardless of his academic ability.	1	2	3	4	5	1	2	3	4	5
r. To encourage mutual trust and respect among faculty, students, and administrators.	1	2	3	4	5	1	2	3	4	5
s. To permit a student wide latitude in selecting the courses he will take toward his degree.	1	2	3	4	5	1	2	3	4	5
t. To provide a wide range of opportunities for specific occupational preparation, e.g., accounting, engineering, pharmacy, etc.	1	2	3	4	5	1	2	3	4	5
u. To provide educational opportunities for adults in the local area.	1	2	3	4	5	1	2	3	4	5
v. To allocate percentages of the total enrollment for minority groups or groups having low socioeconomic status.	1	2	3	4	5	1	2	3	4	5

continued

		This Goal Is Presently—				In the Coming Decade, This Goal Should Be—				
Goal Statement	*Emphasized very strongly*	*Emphasized strongly*	*Emphasized a little*	*Emphasized hardly at all*	*Emphasized not at all*	*Of extremely high importance*	*Of high importance*	*Of medium importance*	*Of low importance*	*Of no importance*
w. To provide a continuing plan of curricular and instructional evaluation for all programs.	1	2	3	4	5	1	2	3	4	5
x. To make financial assistance available to any student who wants to enroll in college.	1	2	3	4	5	1	2	3	4	5
y. To help students develop a respect for their own abilities and an understanding of their limitations.	1	2	3	4	5	1	2	3	4	5
z. To be responsive to the needs of the local community.	1	2	3	4	5	1	2	3	4	5

3. In what community setting is your campus located? Check one.

1. _____ Urban-inner city
2. _____ Urban-ring (suburbs to metropolitan area)
3. _____ Small self-contained communities (independent of any large metropolitan area)
4. _____ Rural

4. How influential is your local district or governing board as compared with state agencies in setting policies for each of the following functions at your college?

Please read each statement. Then put your answer on the appropriate line for each of the three columns specified.

Answer Choice
1 = Fully local
2 = Primarily local, some state
3 = About equal
4 = Primarily state, some local
5 = Fully state

	Five years ago	*Present*	*Five years from now*
a. Breadth and content of curriculum	_____	_____	_____
b. Texts and instuctional materials	_____	_____	_____
c. Minimum standards for probation and retention of students	_____	_____	_____
d. District formation and boundaries	_____	_____	_____
e. Changes in the formal organization	_____	_____	_____
f. Student fees and/or tuition	_____	_____	_____
g. Size of operating and capital budgets	_____	_____	_____
h. Content of operating and capital budgets	_____	_____	_____
i. Staff qualifications	_____	_____	_____
j. Appointments and retention of staff	_____	_____	_____
k. Staff dismissal	_____	_____	_____
l. Long-range planning	_____	_____	_____
m. Specification of educational facilities	_____	_____	_____
n. Admissions policy	_____	_____	_____

5. If your college currently involved in a communication linkup with other institutions for the purposes of sharing information in areas of common interest (e.g., League for Innovation in Community Colleges, G. T. '70, I/D/E/A, etc.)?

   1. _____ Yes   2. _____ No.   3. If yes, please name the specific program(s)

_____

6. Does your institution assist or require faculty to participate in in-service training programs?

   1. _____ Yes   2. _____ No.

   If yes, which of the following training activities are applicable to your institution? (Check all that apply.)

   a. _____ Seminars and workshops (on-campus)   b. _____ Seminars and workshops (off-campus)

c. _____ Enrollment for credit at a university

d. _____ Attendance at professional society meetings

e. _____ Relevant work experience

f. _____ Sabbatical leaves

g. _____ Faculty fellowships (e.g., release time to conduct a research project)

h. _____ Tuition reimbursement

i. _____ Professional travel

7. In general for a new faculty member to be hired for the programs specified below, he must have the following credentials (Circle number corresponding to requirement under each program. If more than one requirement, circle all that apply.):

	Vocational or technical	Adult education	Community services	Academic
No degree required	1	1	1	1
Relevant work experience	2	2	2	2
Two-year degree	3	3	3	3
Four-year degree	4	4	4	4
MA or equivalent	5	5	5	5
PhD or equivalent	6	6	6	6

8. Does your annual budget provide for research, development, or demonstration programs?

   1. _____ Yes   2. _____ No

9. A number of college presidents have felt it of sufficient importance to appoint a full-time "change agent" responsible for stimulating others to update their instructional practices, management skills, curriculum offerings, etc. Is anyone on your immediate staff charged with such a full-time responsibility?

   1. _____ Yes   2. _____ No   If yes, what is his title?

10. In determining the amount of money that will be available to your institution for your annual operating budget during the

next fiscal year, are you required to submit a detailed budget request?

1. _____ Yes   2. _____ No

If no, is your budget predetermined by an outside agency (e.g., state, county, or district office)?

1. _____ Yes   2. _____ No

If yes, please indicate how important the various considerations are that are listed below? (Circle appropriate number under rating for each consideration.)

	Very important	Fairly important	Somewhat important	Not too important	Not at all important	Not available
a. Last year's budget request	1	2	3	4	5	6
b. Last year's actual allocation	1	2	3	4	5	6
c. Overall district priorities (applicable to multiunit district only)	1	2	3	4	5	6
d. Institutional goals and objectives	1	2	3	4	5	6
e. Anticipated funds available	1	2	3	4	5	6
f. Faculty salaries and fringe benefits	1	2	3	4	5	6
g. Administrative staff and fringe benefits	1	2	3	4	5	6
h. Projected FTE enrollments	1	2	3	4	5	6
i. Present and past enrollments	1	2	3	4	5	6
j. Curriculum offerings	1	2	3	4	5	6
k. Student/faculty ratio	1	2	3	4	5	6
l. Faculty strengths	1	2	3	4	5	6
m. Program effectiveness	1	2	3	4	5	6
n. State master plan	1	2	3	4	5	6
o. Student demands	1	2	3	4	5	6
p. Community demands	1	2	3	4	5	6
q. Ratio of residential to nonresidential students	1	2	3	4	5	6

11. In most colleges, budgets have traditionally been established by line item object of expenditure. Some institutions have begun utilizing a planning, programming, budgeting (PPB) system. Has your college converted to a PPB system? (Please check only one of the following.)

1. _____ Yes   2. _____ In process   3. _____ Anticipate doing so
4. _____ Do not anticipate doing so

12. Over the next 10 years, which of the following sources of funds do you expect to utilize in meeting your annual operating budget? (Circle number under degree for each source.)

	Degree utilized				
	Exclusively	*Heavily*	*Moderately*	*Lightly*	*Not at all*
a. Federal government revenues	1	2	3	4	5
b. State government revenues	1	2	3	4	5
c. Shared federal and state revenues distributed by the state	1	2	3	4	5
d. Local property tax	1	2	3	4	5
e. Local bonding	1	2	3	4	5
f. Local sales or income tax	1	2	3	4	5
g. Student tuition and fees	1	2	3	4	5
h. Donations and gifts	1	2	3	4	5
i. Church support	1	2	3	4	5
j. Endowments	1	2	3	4	5
k. Interest on investments	1	2	3	4	5
l. Revenues from profit-making ventures (e.g., publications, bookstores, etc.)	1	2	3	4	5
m. Other categories (please specify) _____	1	2	3	4	5

_____

_____

_____

_____

_____

13. Is the faculty at your college represented by a collective bargaining agent?

1. _____ No. If yes, which of the following (please check):
2. _____ National Faculty Association (an NEA or local affiliate)
3. _____ State Faculty Association
4. _____ American Federation of Teachers (AFL-CIO or local affiliate)
5. _____ American Association of University Professors
6. _____ Other _____

14. Many students are demanding greater voice in how their colleges are run. At this institution, in your opinion, when it comes to matters of college policy, students—
(Please respond to both categories by circling appropriate number in column and row.)

	Do have—					Should have—				
	Full responsibility	*Considerable responsibility*	*Some responsibility*	*Little responsibility*	*No responsibility*	*Full responsibility*	*Considerable responsibility*	*Some responsibility*	*Little responsibility*	*No responsibility*
a. Housing rules and regulations	1	2	3	4	5	1	2	3	4	5
b. Grading practices	1	2	3	4	5	1	2	3	4	5
c. What courses should be offered	1	2	3	4	5	1	2	3	4	5
d. What content should be in those courses	1	2	3	4	5	1	2	3	4	5
e. Hiring new faculty	1	2	3	4	5	1	2	3	4	5
f. Faculty promotion, tenure	1	2	3	4	5	1	2	3	4	5
g. Selection of administrative officers	1	2	3	4	5	1	2	3	4	5
h. Allocation of finances	1	2	3	4	5	1	2	3	4	5
i. Admissions	1	2	3	4	5	1	2	3	4	5
j. Discipline in academic matters (for example, cheating)	1	2	3	4	5	1	2	3	4	5
k. Discipline in social matters (for example, drinking)	1	2	3	4	5	1	2	3	4	5
l. Faculty dismissal	1	2	3	4	5	1	2	3	4	5
m. Required attendance	1	2	3	4	5	1	2	3	4	5
n. Graduation requirements	1	2	3	4	5	1	2	3	4	5
o. Student activity budget	1	2	3	4	5	1	2	3	4	5

15. A number of community or junior colleges have tried or put to work one or more of the following "new" practices.

Please indicate the response which best represents the status of this practice at your institution by putting the appropriate number on the line in front of each of the practices listed below.

Answer Choice
1 = Widespread practice
2 = Limited practice
3 = Not in practice at this time, but planned
4 = Tried it but dropped it
5 = Not in practice nor planned

—— a. Continuous progress program—a program in which students proceed without regard to grade level or sequence; subjects or courses are not divided into quarters or semesters and students progress on an individual basis.

___ b.   **Team teaching**—an arrangement whereby two or more faculty members from the same or different departments, in order to take advantage of their respective competencies, plan, instruct, and evaluate, in one or more subject areas, a group of students.

___ c.   **Student tutoring**—involvement of students in tutoring other students on a volunteer or paid basis at the college.

___ d.   **Instructional aides**—full or part-time paraprofessional persons or students used to assist faculty in essentially nonteaching duties—primarily mechanical tasks such as paper work.

___ e.   **Performance contracting**—contractual relationship with outside organization or faculty group to conduct specified instructional activities leading to prespecified measurable changes in student performance.

___ f.   **Ability grouping**—system in which each student is tested in each subject and then is assigned to the class or subgroup within a class which takes account of his knowledge or ability without regard to the grade to which he was last promoted.

___ g.   **Extended school year**—total number of days students attend school (exclusive of summer sessions) about 200 days or more, or at least approximately two weeks in excess of what is usually required for credit.

___ h.   **Credit by examination**—receiving course credit (for any course) by passing examinations or otherwise demonstrating competence without formally taking the course.

___ i.   **Modular calendar**—breaking up courses into variable length time segments, e.g., 3, 6, 12 weeks, etc., rather than traditional semester or year.

___ j.   **Elimination of letter grades**—reducing present system of five or more letter grades to only two marks—"pass" or "fail."

___ k.   **Flexible scheduling**—operating on a variable schedule which starts with modules of 5 to 20 minutes and organizes the day into various combinations of these modules according to different learning environments needed.

— l. **Individually prescribed instruction**—programs tailored to fit the instructional needs of each student. Monitoring of student progress may or may not involve a computer.

—m. **Independent study**—reading and laboratory work done on student's own, to allow him to experience a variety of learning activities away from the constant supervision of teachers.

— n. **Programmed instruction**—a course designed for independent study in which students regularly use programmed materials so that they can proceed in small steps, respond to information, and are informed immediately whether or not the response is correct.

— o. **Television instruction**—one or more classes regularly using open or closed-circuit television as means of teaching course.

— p. **Simulation or gaming**—one or more classes periodically using a device to create realistic political or social situation in class for helping students to become involved in decision-making.

— q. **Multimedia instruction**—the use of a variety of audiovisual aids by instructors and/or students.

— r. **Behavioral objectives**—specification of curriculum or learning objectives in operational terms, usually accompanied by some specific standard of performance which the student must achieve.

— s. **Learning teams**—small groups of faculty and students getting together to jointly plan and carry out an agreed-upon program of study.

— t. **Advance study for high school students**—an arrangement whereby local high school students can enroll in community or junior college courses.

— u. **Area vocational training for local high schools**—use of a community or junior college facility as an area center for vocational training.

16. In the light of present day college unrest, is your Board of Trustees taking greater, about the same, or less interest than in

the past in the demands posed by the following groups? (Circle appropriate number in column and row.)

	Less interest	*About the same*	*More interest*
a. Faculty	1	2	3
b. Students	1	2	3
c. Administration	1	2	3
d. Local community groups	1	2	3
e. State representatives	1	2	3

In order for the Project Focus staff to keep track of who has or has not completed this questionnaire, we would appreciate your signing and indicating your title. Thank you for your participation. Please be assured that your responses will be held in confidence. A preaddressed, stamped envelope has been provided for returning the document.

(print)   Name

(print)   Title or Position

(print)   Name of Institution

Exhibit IV

Project Focus: Strategies for Change

Madison Office Building
Suite 600
1155 15th Street, N.W.
Washington, D.C. 20005

Area Code 202/833-1177

Edmund J. Gleazer, Jr.
Project Director

David S. Bushnell
Research Director

Francis C. Pray
Associate

March, 1971

Dear Coordinator:

The following questions are designed to help us identify certain trends now underway in colleges throughout the country. The information requested is not available in this form from any other information source. Please be as factual as possible. If the requested information is not available or if it is not applicable, please indicate this in writing on the questionnaire. Please remember, your institution is one of a limited number of institutions selected to participate in this survey. Therefore, your full cooperation is very inportant. All data will be treated with the utmost confidentiality.

If any of the questions are ambiguous, please do not hesitate to call us collect at the following number for clarification—Area Code 202-833-1177.

Thank you for your assistance.

Sincerely,

David S. Bushnell
Research Director

Ivars Zageris
Research Associate

A National Study by the American Association of Junior Colleges under a Grant from the W. K. Kellogg Foundation.

PROJECT FOCUS INSTITUTIONAL QUESTIONNAIRE

Name of Institution ————————————————————————————

Name of Person
completing the
form   ————————————————————————————

Title   ————————————————————————————

Address   ————————————————————————————

Phone Number   ————————————————————————————
                        Area Code   Number   Extension

Did your president review the completed questionnaire?

                              1. Yes———   2. No———

1. Please indicate the projected enrollment at your campus for the
   academic year, 1974-75 and 1979-80. Also, please provide your
   last year's enrollment figures.

	1969-70	*1974-75*	*1979-80*
a) Full-time (with no part-time enrollment considered)	————	————	————
b) Full-time (with part-time enrollment converted into full-time equivalents)*	————	————	————
c) Part-time	————	————	————

What method does your institution use to convert part-time enrollment
figures into full-time equivalents?

*The U.S. Office of Education in their HEGIS Survey recommend the Adjusted
Headcount Method. The full-time equivalent enrollment equals the headcount
of full-time students plus one-third the headcount of part-time students.

2. Approximately what percentage of your freshmen for the academic year 1969-70 entered your institution directly from high school? _____

3. What percentage of your freshmen in the academic year 1969-70 required financial aid?

Estimate % Requiring	*Minority Freshmen*	*All Freshmen*
a) No aid	_____	_____
b) Part aid	_____	_____
c) Full aid	_____	_____

4. At your campus, which of the following programs are available? Please circle the appropriate response. Indicate the number of students (full time equivalents) that were enrolled in the particular programs during the academic year, 1969-70.

Programs	*Yes*	*No*	*Number Enrolled 1969-70*
a) Academic	1	2	_____
b) Occupational (2 year associate degree in applied arts)	1	2	_____
c) Certificate (1 year more or less for specific skill area, e.g., LPN, teacher aide, etc.)	1	2	_____
d) Continuing Education (Adult, special interest courses)	1	2	_____
e) General Education (differentiate from a. and b.)	1	2	_____
f) Developmental, Preparatory, or Remedial	1	2	_____

5. The following questions pertain to the degree of mobility of students within the two-year curriculum. Please answer all four questions by circling the appropriate number for each.

	0% to 19%	20% to 39%	40% to 59%	60% to 79%	80% to 100%
a) Approximately what percent of the full-time students that started the 1969-70 academic year are now sophomores?	1	2	3	4	5
b) Approximately what percent of the full-time freshmen in the academic curriculum that began in 1969-70 have remained in that curriculum	1	2	3	4	5
c) Approximately what percent of the full-time freshmen in the vocational curriculum that began in 1969-70 have remained in that curriculum?	1	2	3	4	5
d) Of those full-time students who did not remain in the academic curriculum, approximately what percent have transferred into other curricular programs?	1	2	3	4	5

6. Which of the following are included in programs and/or services for the disadvantaged? Please circle the appropriate answer.

	Yes	No
a) Recruitment teams	1	2
b) Community contacts for "leads" to disadvantaged students.	1	2
c) Lower admissions requirements	1	2
d) Extra counseling and guidance	1	2
e) Special tutoring: (If YES, please identify the kinds of persons utilized as tutors)		

continued

	Yes	No
Regular faculty	1	2
Special faculty	1	2
Regular students	1	2
Advanced students in disadvantaged programs	1	2

f) Programmed instruction — 1 2
g) Reduced course loads — 1 2
h) Liberalized probationary or readmission practices — 1 2
i) Instruction in development of study skills — 1 2
j) Special courses in ethnic studies — 1 2
k) Stress on Communication skills:
  (If YES, please indicate particular area)

Reading	1	2
Writing	1	2
Speaking	1	2
Listening	1	2
English as a second language	1	2
Understanding of student's own dialect as a language system	1	2

l) Financial aid:
  (If YES, please indicate source and type) — 1 2

	Scholarship	Guaranteed loan	Work Study	Co-op	Other
Federal	1	2	3	4	5
State	1	2	3	4	5
Institutional	1	2	3	4	5
Private	1	2	3	4	5

7. In your judgement, what is likely to happen to the percentage of minority students entering your institution over the next three years? Please check one answer only.

_____ 1) Substantially increase
_____ 2) Remain the same
_____ 3) Increase some
_____ 4) Decrease some
_____ 5) Substantially decrease

8. Please indicate what percent of the total annual operating budget

was expended on the following items during the last five academic years? (The columns should sum to 100%.)

	1965-66	*1966-67*	*1967-68*	*1968-69*	*1969-70*
a) Faculty salaries (exclude administrators)	___	___	___	___	___
b) Physical plant maintenance and operation	___	___	___	___	___
c) Student personnel services	___	___	___	___	___
d) Library services	___	___	___	___	___
e) Housing & food services	___	___	___	___	___
f) Scholarships & loans	___	___	___	___	___
g) Other	___	___	___	___	___
	100%	100%	100%	100%	100%

9. Which of the following are required for admission to your institution? (Please check *all* that apply)

_____ 1. High school diploma or equivalent
_____ 2. Minimum age (_____)
_____ 3. High school grade average (_____)
_____ 4. Test scores
_____ 5. Interview
_____ 6. Letter of recommendation
_____ 7. Physical examination
_____ 8. Other (please specify)

10. What percentage of your students do not meet regular admissions requirements?

_____ 1) None
_____ 2) 0.1-5.0%
_____ 3) 5.1-10.0%
_____ 4) More than 10%

11. Does your institution systematically coordinate with or contact other institutions or programs in order to avoid unnecessary

duplication of course offerings? Please circle one number for each item listed.

	Not applicable	Frequent contact	Infrequent contact	No contact
a) Other community or junior colleges	0	1	2	3
b) Area-vocational schools	0	1	2	3
c) High schools	0	1	2	3
d) Public-technical institutions	0	1	2	3
e) Proprietary schools	0	1	2	3
f) Four-year colleges or universities	0	1	2	3
g) Job-corp centers	0	1	2	3
h) MDTA-skill centers	0	1	2	3
i) Work-incentive programs (WIN)	0	1	2	3
j) Neighborhood-youth corps	0	1	2	3
k) Concentrated-employment programs (CEP)	0	1	2	3
l) Industrial-training programs (offered by private industry)	0	1	2	3
m) Others (please specify)	0	1	2	3

12. During the last three academic years, how many students of the following ethnic groups were enrolled in the programs mentioned below? Please note the full-and-part-time breakdown.

U.S. Citizens or Permanent Residents

Academic Year	Enrolled In	American Indian		Black or Negro		Oriental		Spanish Surnamed American		All Other U.S. Students		All Foreign Students		Grand Total
		F-T	P-T	F-T	P-T	F-T	P-T	F-T	P-T	F-T	P-T	F-T	P-T	
1967-68	Occupational Programs													
	Academic Programs													
	All Programs													
1968-69	Occupational Programs													
	Academic Programs													
	All Programs													
1969-70	Occupational Programs													
	Academic Programs													
	All Programs													

Appendix C.
Innovative
Institutions Index

One of the efforts of this study was to rank-order the institutions by their degree of "innovativeness." "Innovativeness" was defined as the willingness of an institution to adopt new techniques in either college administration or teaching methods.

Operationally, the following method was employed to rank the institutions. Dr. Gleazer, who visited 21 of the institutions with completed presidents' questionnaires, was asked to rate the "innovativeness" of these institutions in terms of his perception of their willingness to change. The scale was from 1 to 4, with 1 being highly innovative and 4 not innovative at all.

It was hypothesized that Questions 5, 6, 7, 9, 11, and 15 of the presidents' questionnaire could be used to predict Dr. Gleazer's evaluation of the innovativeness of the 21 schools. The questions used were as follows:

Question #15

(a) Delete "u," leaving 20 possible entries.
(b) Establish scale as follows:

100 points ◄─────────────────► 20 points
Not versatile at all in   Highly versatile in

| regards to teaching methods and administrative procedures. | regards to teaching methods and administrative procedures. |

Questions #5, 8, and 9

(a) Yes—1 point   (b) No—4 points

Question #6

(a) If yes, 7 to 9 checked, 1 point
            4 to 6 checked, 2 points
            1 to 3 checked, 3 points

(b) If no, 4 points

Question #11

(a) Yes—1 point
(b) In process—2 points
(c) Anticipate doing so—3 points
(d) Do not anticipate doing so—4 points

It was anticipated that Dr. Gleazer's evaluation = f [New teaching practices (#15), change agent at institution (#9), communication linkup with other institutions (#5), having PPB System at institution (#11), having budget for research and development (#8), and faculty training programs (#6)].

A stepwise regression analysis was applied. Having entered all the variables, the multiple correlation coefficient was determined to be 0.813. However, questions #11, 8, and 6 did not contribute significantly to predicting Dr. Gleazer's evaluations. Using only questions #15, 9, and 5, the multiple correlation coefficient was 0.804.

The summary statistics were as follows:

Multiple Correlation Coefficient   0.804   (Adjusted R   = 0.779)
F for analysis of Variable (D.F. = 3.17) 10.354
Standard Error of Estimate   0.745   (Adjusted SE = 0.785)

VARIABLE	REGULAR COEF.	STD. ERROR COEF.	COMPUTED T	BETA COEF.
# 9	0.38546	0.14362	2.684	0.50779
# 5	0.23254	0.11654	1.995	0.30915
#15	0.02500	0.01963	1.273	0.25344
INTERCEPT	−0.04191			

Thus, the formula for determining the degree of innovativeness is

Degree of innovativeness =

−0.04191 + 0.38546 (#9) + 0.23254 (#5) + 0.02500 (#15).

Appendix D.
Perceptions of Goals for the 70s

TABLE D-1 *Presidents' perceptions of goals for the 1970s*

Goal	Output or process goal	Public Present Rank	Public Present $\bar{X}$	Public Preferred Rank	Public Preferred $\bar{X}$	Private Present Rank	Private Present $\bar{X}$	Private Preferred Rank	Private Preferred $\bar{X}$
Serve higher education needs of youth from local community	O	1	1.23	1	1.13	4	1.95	10	1.75
Respond to needs of local community	O	2	1.62	2	1.23	11	2.45	12	1.85
Encourage mutual trust and respect among faculty, students, and administrators	P	3	1.71	4	1.29	1	1.70	1	1.15
Make financial assistance available to any academically qualified student	P	4	1.74	6	1.34	8	2.20	7	1.60

| Goal | Output or process goal | Public | | | | Private | | | |
| | | Present | | Preferred | | Present | | Preferred | |
		Rank	$\bar{X}$	Rank	$\bar{X}$	Rank	$\bar{X}$	Rank	$\bar{X}$
Provide educational opportunities for adults in the local area	P	5	1.83	8	1.36	20	3.10	14	2.11
Establish and define institutional purposes	P	6	1.83	5	1.31	2	1.75	2	1.15
Provide wide range of opportunities for specific occupational preparation	P	7	1.97	12	1.49	18	2.95	21	2.50
Help students respect own abilities and limitations	O	8	2.01	11	1.41	3	1.80	5	1.32
Help students adapt to new occupational requirements	O	9	2.04	3	1.27	10	2.45	13	1.90
Maintain an atmosphere of intellectual excitement on campus	P	10	2.04	10	1.39	6	2.05	4	1.20
Make financial assistance available to any student who wants to enroll	P	11	2.07	13	1.57	15	2.70	19	2.37
Provide some form of education for any student regardless of academic ability	P	12	2.14	14	1.64	21	3.10	24	2.70
Ensure faculty participation in institutional decision making	P	13	2.19	19	1.94	9	2.35	9	1.75
Provide for curricular and instructional evaluation	P	14	2.32	7	1.35	7	2.15	6	1.40
Experiment with new forms of instruction	P	15	2.36	15	1.69	12	2.50	8	1.75

TABLE D-1 (Continued)

| Goal | Output or process goal | Public | | | | Private | | | |
| | | Present | | Preferred | | Present | | Preferred | |
		Rank	$\overline{X}$	Rank	$\overline{X}$	Rank	$\overline{X}$	Rank	$\overline{X}$
Reeducate and retrain those whose vocational capabilities are obsolete	O	16	2.43	9	1.38	25	3.75	22	2.52
Develop programs for the special student, e.g., disadvantaged, bright, foreign	P	17	2.53	18	1.73	19	3.00	18	2.35
Encourage students to undertake self-directed study	O	18	2.54	16	1.69	14	2.68	11	1.84
Ensure student participation in institutional decision making	P	19	2.57	22	2.17	13	2.65	15	2.20
Increase number and diversity of sources of income	P	20	2.59	17	1.69	5	1.95	3	1.15
Attract representative number of minority faculty members	P	21	2.74	23	2.26	23.5	3.55	23	2.65
Permit student wide latitude in course selection	P	22	2.86	21	2.10	17	2.85	17	2.30
Help solve social, economic, or political problems in the immediate geographical area	O	23	3.03	24	2.29	22	3.32	20	2.44
Help formulate programs in a number of public policy areas, e.g., pollution control	O	24	3.04	20	2.03	23.5	3.55	25	2.75
Allocate % of enrollment for minority groups or those of low socio-economic status	P	25	3.64	25	3.30	26	4.00	26	3.32
Strengthen religious faith of students	O	26	4.09	26	3.71	16	2.80	16	2.25

TABLE D-2   *Faculty perceptions of goals for the 1970s*

| | Public | | | | Private | | | |
| | Present | | Preferred | | Present | | Preferred | |
Goal	Rank	$\overline{X}$	Rank	$\overline{X}$	Rank	$\overline{X}$	Rank	$\overline{X}$
Serve higher education needs of youth from local community	1	1.60	2	1.41	3	2.28	4	1.85
Provide some form of education for any student regardless of academic ability	2	1.64	7	1.74	2	2.28	9	2.35
Respond to needs of local community	3	1.93	4	1.52	7	2.58	5	2.00
Help students adapt to new occupational requirements	4	2.08	3	1.44	6	2.53	3	1.77
Make financial assistance available to any student who wants to enroll	5	2.20	9	1.86	5	2.44	6	2.12
Help students respect own abilities and limitations	6	2.25	1	1.40	1	2.14	1	1.35
Reeducate and retrain those whose vocational capabilities are obsolete	7	2.30	5	1.54	11	3.64	10	2.45
Ensure faculty participation in institutional decision making	8	2.60	6	1.61	4	2.37	2	1.66
Attract representative number of minority faculty members	9	2.82	11	2.47	12	3.66	11	2.71
Ensure student participation in institutional decision making	10	2.86	10	2.31	8	2.71	8	2.23
Help formulate programs in a number of public policy areas, e.g., pollution control	11	2.90	8	1.83	9	3.15	7	2.20
Allocate percent of enrollment for minority groups or those of low socioeconomic status	12	3.10	12	2.80	10	3.33	12	2.93

Index